PRAISE FOR *SEE ME AFTER CLASS*

Take it from the professionals who know...

"As any mentor of new teachers will tell you, when working with new teachers you need to have empathy and be able to show them that others have gone there before them and survived the trial by fire. You need to have a great sense of humor to lighten the moment when things get tough. And you need to have tried-and-tested tools and tips to offer to help them plot a path forward in their classrooms. *See Me After Class* has all of those components and is a valuable addition to the resource library for new teachers and for those who work with them."

—Ellen Moir, Founder and CEO of The New Teacher Center

"...a useful, empathetic guide to weathering the first-year lumps...a frothy, satisfying Guinness for the teacher's soul."

—Dan Brown, NBCT, Director of the Future Educators Association, and author of *The Great Expectations School*

"Roxanna Elden is one of the most practical, engaging, and entertaining writers on education issues around. *See Me After Class* is a must-have book for any teacher's bookshelf. On second-thought, you'll probably want to keep it on your classroom desk since you'll use it so much!"

—Larry Ferlazzo, teacher and author of *Helping Students Motivate Themselves*

"With disarming humor, Elden's supremely practical book includes firsthand accounts from the trenches and helps new recruits figure out what no college prep class taught."

—*American Teacher Journal*

"This is the kind of no-nonsense straight talk that teachers are starved for, but too rarely get. I sure wish this had been available when I was a new teacher. Roxanna Elden tells it like it is, with a heavy dose of practicality, a dash of cynicism, a raft of constructive suggestions, and plenty of wry humor. I recommend *See Me After Class*, wholeheartedly and unabashedly."

—Rick Hess, Director of Education Policy Studies at AEI, author of *Education Week* blog "Rick Hess Straight Up"

"A grab bag of advice, anecdotes, horror stories, and tales of triumph, *See Me After Class* offers straightforward professional advice with a wry twist."

—*One Day Magazine*

"Without any sugarcoating, Roxanna deals with the challenges that educators face day-in and day-out through insights and stories from long-time educators as well as her own experiences."

—Teacherscount.org

"A great idea for required reading in teacher education classes."

—Shawn Denight, Florida Teacher of the Year

See Me After Class

SECOND EDITION

ADVICE FOR
TEACHERS
BY
TEACHERS

ROXANNA ELDEN

Published by Sourcebooks, Inc.
P.O. Box 4410, Naperville, Illinois 60567-4410
(630) 961-3900
Fax: (630) 961-2168
www.sourcebooks.com

Originally published in New York by Kaplan Publishing in 2011

Library of Congress Cataloging-in-Publication data is on file with the publisher.

Printed and bound in the United States of America.
VP 10 9 8 7 6 5 4 3

To my mother, for making me a writer
To my students, for making me a teacher
(except a few of you and you know who you are)

CONTENTS

1
WHAT THIS BOOK IS...AND IS NOT

Some teachers are naturals from the first day. They instinctively motivate students, set high expectations, and manage—not discipline—their classes. They stay positive and organized, tracking progress in binders of color-coded data and planning lessons that address each child's unique learning modality. These teachers don't just teach—they inspire! They spring out of bed each morning knowing materials are laid out, papers are graded, and their classrooms are welcoming environments where all students can succeed. This book is not for them.

This book is for anyone who wishes those teachers would stop telling you how organized they are while you stare at a growing stack of ungraded essays. It's for those of you who are sleeping less than ever before, raising your voices louder than you ever imagined you would, and wondering why kids take sooooo long in the bathroom and often come out covered in water. This is for any new teacher wondering whether to get out of bed at all.

Read this when a lesson goes horribly wrong, when your whole class "forgets" a major project, or when a parent curses at you in front of the kids. Pull it out at lunch on a bad day or on Sunday night as you battle those six-more-hours-till-Monday stomach cramps. This is meant to get you to school *tomorrow*.

But first, a few warnings…

THIS BOOK IS NOT PROFESSIONAL DEVELOPMENT

No book can replace the difficult, necessary process of learning to teach. Read this after you have attended more than enough workshops, received so many lists of recommended books you get tired from reading the lists, and gotten plenty of advice about time-consuming things you could do to be a better teacher. I'm assuming you've heard the terms *benchmark, classroom management,* and *data-driven instruction*. You also know which of these describes what you were doing wrong when your principal walked in.

You may even be enrolled in a certification program, where you spend some of the longest hours of your life watching PowerPoint presentations on the importance of hands-on lessons, taking multiple-choice practice tests, and praying this isn't how your students feel while you're teaching.

This book is meant to keep you from getting discouraged when it seems like all those fabulous ideas you learned in training don't work in your own classroom: no one understands the directions, it turns out you had no business giving those kids glue in the first place, and it also turns out the *National Geographic* magazines you found cheap and felt great about became a gallery of nude pictures for your sixth-graders. It's also for the next day, when parents show up to complain—even though their kids are downloading much more graphic pictures on their home computers and bringing them to school…which is why their printers ran out of ink…which is why their projects aren't finished.

You, on the other hand, still have to prepare that sample hands-on lesson plan for your training class tonight.

THIS BOOK IS NOT *CHICKEN SOUP FOR THE TEACHER'S SOUL*

It's more like *Hard Liquor for the Teacher's Soul*—new teachers need something stronger than chicken soup. Read this on the days when any book by a teacher who taught kids to play violin during lunch or took busloads of perfectly behaved fifth-graders on a tour of college campuses makes you want to beat your head against the wall until pieces of scalp and hair are all over the place.

The basis for this book is an idea that worked for me: teachers willing to admit their mistakes are much more helpful to rookies than those who say, "Well, they would know better than to do that in *my* class." The stories in this book should be bad enough to make you feel better.

The real reason to feel better, though, is that all the people who shared their stories in this book went on to become successful, experienced teachers. They're not administrators (who, don't get me wrong, do important jobs). They're not counselors (who also do important jobs). They're not presenters or auditors from a downtown office (who do...jobs).

They are teachers. In classrooms. And they love it—most days.

THIS BOOK IS NOT *TEACHING FOR DUMMIES*

Dummies shouldn't be teachers. As a country, we need educators who have brains, dedication, enthusiasm, and common sense. We need people who want to change things in the schools where things most need to change.

But we need you to stay at your jobs, and stay sane.

Acting like a hard job can be done easily is a sure way to do it wrong. The knowledge teachers need is complicated, it's important, and it's way more than anyone can learn in one year. The great teachers of the future know they're not great yet. They know they're making mistakes, and some of those mistakes are big. They're sorting through a million pieces of advice, each starting with the words "All you have to do is…," until they want to lie on their backs in the school hallway and yell, "This is all the time and energy I have! Can someone please tell me what I should really spend it on?"

If you can relate to the preceding paragraph, you were my inspiration. And this book is for you.

2

THE TEN THINGS YOU WILL WISH SOMEONE HAD TOLD YOU

If someone had told me everything I needed to know before I started teaching, it wouldn't have mattered. I wouldn't have listened anyway. I was better and knew more than anyone. I was exactly the kind of new teacher I'd like to help. Talk about irony—I wouldn't have listened to myself even after I had been through the school of hard knocks. Still, maybe other new teachers aren't as stubborn and hardheaded as I was.

—16-year teacher

Don't misunderstand. We need to be stubborn. If you've watched any movies about inspiring teachers, you know part of our job description is making the impossible possible—and that's just before lunch.

But then we need to line up the class for lunch, and someone in back keeps pushing, which makes other kids whine, and you can't tell who's talking in the front, but one of his or her friends just started kicking the door, and the noise level keeps going up until, "THERE IS NO WAY WE ARE LEAVING THIS CLASS-ROOM UNTIL YOU CAN LINE UP THE RIGHT WAY!" Hey. That wasn't in the script.

It's important to set the bar high in education, but as a new teacher, I was desperate for someone to break the "stay positive" code and say, "Yes, this happens in my classroom too. There are no easy answers, but here's how I deal with it." I was waiting for others to admit they had doubted their own abilities, made their own mistakes. I am still waiting to see an "inspiring teacher" movie in which the teacher actually grades papers.

In interviews for this book, there were ten main things teachers wished someone had told them earlier. No doubt you have heard some of these, but they are worth repeating. If you haven't heard them all, you will be glad you're hearing them now.

1. A Lot of the "Advice" You Get Will Make You Feel Worse, Not Better

❝*I went to an in-service where the presenter said, 'Well, we all know yelling doesn't work,' like it was the most obvious thing in the world. I saw other teachers nodding, even some who I had heard screaming at their students. At that point in the year, the only way I could get my class's attention was by yelling at the top of my lungs. I had to yell louder and louder as time went on until I was losing my voice. I asked a teacher with a perfectly behaved class how she got kids to be quiet without screaming. All she said was 'They know I mean business.'***❞**

You will hear lots of advice your first year. Some will be good, but that doesn't mean you can put it into practice right away. Some will be bad, but you won't realize that until you have more experience. Either way, advice will come from three main sources:

- **Professional development**   As you attend training sessions, you will learn that if your students are not using "learning logs," your entire year may be a waste of time. Some of the kids may even "unlearn" everything they have learned in their lives. No, wait! Kids can't understand what they read unless you have done pre-reading activities with manipulatives. No, sorry, that's wrong too. Research has shown that any sentence beginning "Research has shown…" can end in many contradictory ways, especially if the presenter is trying to sell products or consulting services to your school.

- **Other teachers**   Experienced teachers generally have the information you need. Unfortunately, some coworkers have trouble explaining their techniques. Others give advice based on what they think they should be doing instead of providing honest answers. This makes you feel inadequate without helping you at all.

- **Non-teachers**   People who work with other adults are eager to tell teachers what they would do if *they* were teachers. After all, they've watched inspiring teacher movies too. This is unfortunate. After a long, unrewarding day of teaching, suggestions like "Let them know you care" or "Try making it fun" from people who've never taught will make you want to rip off your head—or theirs—and roll it down the street like a bowling ball. Remember, they mean well.

2. Your Classroom Is Your First Responsibility

66 *To prove myself, I signed up to teach night school, tutored on Saturdays, and sponsored the volleyball team. I was at school for twelve hours on a short day and still had to bring papers home. I spread myself so thin I was ineffective in everything.* **99**

Unless you were specifically hired to run a program or coach, don't take on other responsibilities until you have a firm grip on teaching. Managing a team or planning a camping trip is beautiful, but these things can become your worst nightmare when grades are due the next day and you still have to track down parents who haven't signed permission slips. Be sure you can walk before you try to run—or before you sign up for anything that involves selling candy bars.

3. You Can't Change Everything Your First Year, and You Shouldn't Try To

"*I've seen some rookies enter the classroom determined to correct all the mistakes committed by teachers before them. They are sure they will fix what is wrong with education. This just isn't gonna happen! If you start out trying to fix every problem, you will quickly burn out. We lose a couple of new teachers every year before Christmas. Sometimes a teacher who came in talking about changing the system will just up and quit during a class—just get up and walk out. This is the worst thing teachers can do to their students.***"**

When I was interviewing teachers for this book, the saying "Pick your battles" came up too many times to count. As a fresh observer, you will certainly notice some imperfections in the way your school operates. You may see some things that are unfair or inefficient, and some that even slap common sense right in the face. Still, resist the urge to fight the system your first year and focus on making yourself the best teacher you can be under the circumstances. Sometimes being a great teacher means learning to function in a dysfunctional environment. Save your fighting strength until you have enough experience to be taken seriously, and until you know which battles to fight.

4. Ask for and Accept Help

"*I thought using the textbook was a sign of laziness, and using other teachers' ideas showed I couldn't think of my own. I believed I was going above and beyond by doing everything myself. In fact, my pride in my originality kept my students from learning everything they could have.***"**

As rookies, we often feel the only way to be a good teacher is to come up with original lessons every night, create all our own worksheets, collect real-world examples of every concept, write reading materials ourselves, or buy books and cover them with homemade paper. While you will probably create some of your own learning tools, be open to using ideas from the professionals around you. If you have textbooks, understand that they, too, are written by professionals who have taught your subject. Use other people's work as a starting point. Creativity and effort are important, but reinventing the wheel is not the best use of either one.

5. Your Students Are Kids, No Matter How Big They Are

66 *This huge, thuggish-looking kid walked into my room like he would just step on me if I told him to do anything. He turned out to be a nice, hardworking student. My biggest behavior problem that year was a kid who was about 4'11".* 99

If you are an average-sized adult in a high school or middle school, expect that some students will be taller, wider, and physically stronger than you. Don't let this intimidate you or make you forget they still need you to teach and care about them. In a well-run classroom, (most) kids will listen to you (most of the time) regardless of their size.

6. You Are Not Your Students' Friend—They Don't Even Have to Like You at First

66 *Everyone tells you not to try to be friends with students, but for many young teachers, it's hard to play the role of a nerdy or uptight adult. At some point, you will be tempted to let classroom management slip because you want kids to like you—or at least recognize you as the cool teacher you know you are.*

Unfortunately, freedom is easier to give than to take away, and getting the students to like you is a losing effort anyway, because they won't ever like you the way they like their friends. You're an authority figure. Act like one, and the kids will grow to respect you and like you—as a teacher. **99**

If you are too worried about students liking you, they will pick up on this and be very sweet at first, then run around your room like animals and cause property damage the rest of the year. You, meanwhile, will turn into the incarnation of evil as you try to tighten the reins. At the end of the year, the kids won't even like you. They will like the teacher who was "too strict" for a few months and had the luxury of showing a human side once things were under control.

7. Make a Schedule for Paperwork

66 *It would have been helpful if I had known to set aside specific times to grade and not think I would 'just get it done.' I didn't. I hate grading, and I need a schedule to force me to do it.* **99**

Beginning teachers often feel they need the entire night to plan the next day's lessons, so ungraded papers can pile up fast. You begin by telling yourself you will catch up over the weekend. Unfortunately, just because you bring student work home doesn't mean it will come back graded. In fact, the larger a pile of paper is, the less you want to deal with it, so you may just spend your weekends staring at it or separating it into smaller piles. Meanwhile, students continue to hand in work. Now throw in some seemingly useless district documentation requirements—due two days ago—and you begin to hear the ticking of a paperwork time bomb. There are two things to remember about paperwork: first, it is a much larger part of your job than you imagined it would be. Second, it is never completely finished. One of the best presents you can give yourself as a teacher is to make a schedule for grading and stick to it.

8. Teaching Is Physically Exhausting

66*At my first job, roosters in the schoolyard made their first noises as I walked into school. For a while, I thought I was waking them up.***99**

As a beginning teacher, you often drive to and from work in the dark. You stay on your feet most of the day. Your remaining energy is drained by anxiety that kids will hurt themselves or others if you turn your head for a second. When you finally get home, all you want to do is sleep, but you have to plan or you won't know what you're doing the next day. You are never really done working. By Friday, you feel like falling asleep on the drive home.

9. Lock Your Door When You Leave the Room

66*Some of the newer teachers at my school leave their doors open because they are 'just stepping out for a minute.' I always warn them a lot can happen in a minute.***99**

Wear your classroom keys around your neck or wrist. If you can't find your keys easily, you'll be tempted to leave your room unlocked. Elementary school teachers probably think this advice applies only to high school. Grade school kids are little and cute, right? They'd be terrified of going into a classroom when they weren't supposed to, right? I mean, it's not like two of your sweetest, best-behaved fourth-graders would sneak out of line at the end of the day, hide in the boys' bathroom, sneak back into the room, open your desk drawer, steal an expensive toy belonging to their classmate, and let you come back into the room with the girl's mother to find a $100 toy inexplicably missing, right? Wrong. Lock your door.

10. Things Will Get Better

❝ *Don't give up on your students. They will grow and mature during the school year. Most important, don't give up on yourself. For whatever reason, you decided to become a teacher. No matter how difficult your teaching assignment is, that reason is still valid. Explain, explain, and explain again. Be patient with your students. Check for their understanding to be sure they are with you. If they don't get it the first time, it doesn't mean you're failing as a teacher. You simply have to keep trying, going, and reflecting—and you will improve. This means your students will improve.* **❞**

At some point during this year, you may wonder whether you would have considered being a teacher if you knew what was ahead of you. The answer is yes. The reason so many people have done this for so many years is that certain moments in this profession more than make up for your worst days. When these moments finally come, you will understand why everything else was worth it.

3

FIRST DAZE

*Y*ou know the first day of school is the most important, right? Of course you know the first day of school is the most important. You received multiple copies of a 337-page book on the importance of the first day of school. You spent months planning for the first day of school and…you messed up the first day of school.

Now what?

This chapter addresses the three questions most new teachers have about the first day of school: "Where do I start?" "What should I expect?" and, most important, "What if my first day doesn't go as planned?" (because it never does).

WHERE YOU START
First-Day Shopping List

The rookie-teacher shopping instinct is to buy every object you might use for any possible lesson you might think of one day. When I cleaned out my fourth-grade classroom, I found a strange collection of toys, magnetic letters, and dollar-store puzzle books, still unopened in a cabinet after two years. I had also spent my own money on supplies the school later gave us for free. Yet my first day I didn't have a stapler or rubber bands—two things I needed badly. The following is a list of supplies you may want in stock before school starts, but check what your school provides before buying anything on your own.

BEFORE-SCHOOL SHOPPING LISTS

Supplies to Buy at a Dollar or Discount Store

Hit the cheap stores first. You will blow a high enough percentage of your puny salary on classroom supplies this year—you don't need the best-quality staples.

- ❏ Manila folders (one for each student and at least 100 extra).
- ❏ Colored computer paper (buy white paper only if your school does not provide it or you have to slay an evil dragon to get 20 sheets of paper).
- ❏ Colored pens for grading.
- ❏ Staplers.
- ❏ Staples.
- ❏ Paper clips.
- ❏ Rubber bands.
- ❏ Sticky notes.
- ❏ Scissors.
- ❏ Sharpies or other permanent markers.
- ❏ Scotch tape.
- ❏ Clear packing tape.
- ❏ A three-hole punch.
- ❏ A digital kitchen timer.
- ❏ Dry-erase markers or chalk for the board.
- ❏ Wet-erase or overhead markers if you use a projector.
- ❏ Chalkboard or markerboard erasers.
- ❏ A spray bottle.
- ❏ Paper towels.
- ❏ Tissues.
- ❏ Hand sanitizer.
- ❏ Spray cleaner or disinfectant wipes.

Supplies to Get at an Office Supply Store

Office supply stores are a little more expensive, but they offer a big, professional-looking selection. Don't forget to ask for your teacher discount.

❏ Anything on the preceding list you couldn't find at other stores.

❏ File boxes (if you have no file drawers or plan to use hanging folders for student work).

❏ Hanging folders (if you buy the file boxes).

❏ Stackable trays to organize incoming papers (at least six if you plan to use the system described in Chapter 5 of this book).

❏ A box of presharpened lotto pencils (to lend to students as needed).

❏ A giant, paper desk calendar that matches the months of the academic year.

Supplies to Get at the Teacher Supply Store

Teacher supply stores are the most expensive, but they sell things you can't find at other stores, like pictures of animals making inspirational statements. Keep in mind that the teacher supply store the week before school starts is like Toys "R" Us on Christmas Eve. It can get ugly.

❏ **Something to cover your walls:** Most schools supply paper for your bulletin boards. Some provide the border that goes around them, but if you want the fancy stuff with pictures on it, you probably have to buy it yourself. You may also want posters or decorations to make your room feel like a real classroom.

❏ **Sticky stuff to put up posters:** Sticking decorations to your classroom walls for the whole year usually takes more than tape. There are many options, but I recommend double-sided foam tape.

❏ **E-Z Grader:** This tool helps you quickly calculate percentages on assignments. It costs about six dollars, and you'll know why it's worth it when you grade your first 17-question quiz.

> ❏ **Stickers:** This is one area where the teacher supply store usually has the best value. You can get packages of 800 stickers for less than five dollars.
>
> ❏ **A whole bunch of other stuff you didn't know you needed:** You'll see what I mean.

What to Include in Your First-Day Lesson Plan

Please don't take your first-day cues from any movie where the teacher stands on a desk. The first day of class should be the most structured day of the year, not the most exciting. It's all about setting the tone so that you can teach with minimum drama the rest of the year. Your first-day lesson plan is really more of a checklist, and it should include the following elements, most of which will take less time than you expect:

❏ Meeting students at the door and quietly directing them to an assigned seat.

❏ Taking attendance and processing no-show students while the class works quietly.

❏ Arranging paperwork for the office while the class works quietly.

❏ Learning as many of your students' names as possible while the class works quietly.

❏ Collecting parent contact information before students realize they don't want you to have their parents' contact information (while the class works quietly).

❏ Explaining expectations to older students and practicing procedures with younger students.

❏ Assigning homework you plan to collect and grade, even if you are only asking students to get papers signed.

Papers You May Want to Give Out the First Day

Student information sheet   Schools require parents to fill out emergency information cards, but you will still want to make a form of your own. Older kids can fill this out in class. Younger students should take it home. This paper should include any information you might want later in the year, like home languages or after-school activities. You should also collect as many forms of parent contact info as possible. You can put these in a binder or tape them to the front of manila folders to create the record files described in Chapter 5.

Student interest survey   The student interest survey serves two purposes. First, it helps you get to know your students as people. Second, it keeps students busy and quiet while you juggle the demands of the first day. Ask questions that require long answers, but don't expect the survey to take up too much time. A two-page survey can take as little as ten minutes.

Parent letter or syllabus   A letter to parents or a syllabus can explain your expectations, rules, supply list, grading scale, and what you plan to cover in the class. Don't go into more detail than you can be sure of. Students should have their parents sign the letter or the last page of the syllabus and return it for a grade.

Supply list   If your list of supplies is too long to include in your parent letter or syllabus, send it separately. Talk to coworkers for an idea of what families are used to sending. For younger grades, include classroom supplies like tissues and hand sanitizer—a class of thirty runny noses and sixty dirty hands goes through these things quickly.

Procedures   Make a list of procedures you expect students to follow. Write at a level they can understand.

Long writing assignment or activity packet   If your students are old
enough to write on their own, have a long writing assignment
prepared for the first day. A well-planned prompt can help you
get to know your students, their writing, and their motivation
levels. More important, it will take up at least half an hour of
class time. If you have other things planned and don't get to it,
that's fine. However, if you are stuck with an empty half hour
after you finish your first-day plans, trust me, you will wish you
had a writing assignment. If students are too young to write,
make an activity packet based on the letters of the alphabet to
keep them coloring for a while.

First-Day Tips from Experienced Teachers

66_Always start tougher than you really want to be. Try to give consequences
early and make an example of the first student who tests a rule. You can always
ease up later, but if you hesitate to give consequences for breaking rules, kids
will sense that._**99**

66 _Try to learn names as soon as possible. You can give students an index card
and ask them to write their names, seat numbers, one identifying detail, and
one thing they would like you to know about them. You can use these to call on
students for the rest of the day and to memorize their names as they work._**99**

66 _If you don't think your class list will be exact, you may want to label desks
with numbers instead of names. I tape playing cards to each desk—ace through
nine of each suit—which divides the class into four teams. When the kids come
in the first day, I hand them a card and say, 'Good morning. Your seat is the
one that matches this card. The rest of the directions are on the board.' I make
seating charts once I know kids better, but this system keeps kids from sitting
with their friends or collecting in the back of the room on the first day._**99**

❝ *Relax, it's the second, third, and fiftieth days you have to worry about.* **❞**

PREPARING YOUR ROOM AND YOURSELF FOR STUDENTS

You may have already had your first totally-unprepared-teacher dream. I still have this dream near the end of every vacation, and most teachers I've discussed it with know exactly what I'm talking about. It changes, of course, but it always goes something like this:

> (Scary music begins.) You have somehow slept through a week's worth of alarm clocks and it is now your first day of school. You get lost or stuck in traffic, so you show up late, and have to walk past your principal in your pajamas/underwear/clothes-you-went-out-in-last-night. Your classroom/subject/class list has been changed without warning, so you walk in completely unprepared to teach a huge rowdy class that includes every bad child you have ever seen—even bullies from your own school days. Then your principal walks in to observe you…
>
> You wake up sweating and realize it was just a dream, but then a thought hits you: school starts in two weeks, and you're *not* prepared. (Scary music returns.) Your to-do list swirls into a mental tornado. How will you find time to finish all this stuff?

Ten-Day Countdown to the First Day of School

Every district has a different time line, but the following example will help you plan your own schedule to make the most of the time you have left.

Ten… Plan your discipline strategy in as much detail as possible, including rules, incentives, and consequences. Type your rules poster and expected classroom procedures. If you feel you don't know exactly what to say, force yourself to type anyway. Revise later. Start avoiding people who say you chose the wrong career or want to explain why they didn't become teachers themselves.

Nine... Write lesson plans for your first week. Once again, they don't have to be perfect. They just have to be *done*.

Eight... Start preparing other classroom forms you think you will need: checklists, signature sheets, and so on. Print your rules poster, along with quotes or pictures you want on your walls.

Seven... See your classroom before the weekend if possible, and find out what supplies your school provides. Check whether you have a working computer and printer in your room and plan accordingly. Get teachers' guides for the textbooks you will be using, and ask for the curriculum you will need to follow, if any. Meet your principal's administrative assistant, who you will probably deal with more often than the principal. Check with him or her to be sure you are on a twelve-month pay schedule, unless you have another way to support yourself over the summer. Meet the other staff who will affect your quality of life: custodians, zone mechanics, and security. Start arranging your furniture and think about how to organize and decorate. Then head to the stores with your first-day shopping lists.

" *I finally made it to room 19, where I flipped the 'call office' button instead of the light switch three times. I found the lights, apologized to the irritated voice coming over the speaker, and looked around the room. It seemed both huge and tiny at the same time, like the length of the school day: huge when I thought about how I would be responsible for filling it, tiny when I thought about how much I would have to fit into it effectively.* **"**

Six... Finish shopping. Laminate your posters. Make sure the room
is arranged the way you want it, and request any furniture you
still need. Then start planning. Add specific textbook pages to
your lesson plans, and collect materials for your first week's
lessons. Use a marker to fill in school holidays and testing dates
on your giant, paper desk calendar. Then, in pencil, try to map
out *very basic* unit plans for your first month.

(Weekend) Try on your first-day outfit. You probably already know
you should dress like the professional that you are, but if you are
just starting to buy teacher clothes, there are a few other things
you should remember. First, find comfortable work shoes!!!
Really. You might not sit down for seven and a half hours. If
your feet have blisters on them after twenty minutes, it will feel
much longer. Second, make sure your clothes cover what you
want them to at all times. Lift up your arms and check your
reflection. Do you see stomach or back? Lean forward in the
mirror. Is this what you want showing when you bend over to
help? If you teach, say, kindergarten, imagine sitting on a chair
while the children sit on the floor listening to you read. Change
outfits as needed.

Five... If you hoped to get lots of productive work done today,
the joke's on you. School districts often schedule new teacher
orientation during the week before school starts. This means
instead of working in your classroom like you want to, you
will spend two days in a downtown auditorium listening to the
various ways you can get fired. A continental breakfast will
be provided.

❝ *The first day of new-teacher orientation, they played a video montage of different teachers in their classrooms with 'Wind Beneath My Wings' playing in
the background; later they played another 'inspirational' montage set to 'I Hope*

You Dance.' All I could think was, 'If I'm able to pass on anything to my stu-
dents, I hope I can train them not to be taken in by such sentimental dreck.' **99**

Four... Continue orientation. If you can't get to school afterward,
prepare as much as possible at home. This is a good day to
create the behind-your-desk filing system described in Chapter
5. Once school starts, setting up files won't feel like much of
a priority.

Three... Prepare to be blindsided with at least one meeting or
training session, but you should still have several hours to work
in your room. The good news is your school is now full of veteran teachers whose ideas you can beg, borrow, and steal. You
should meet your mentor teacher and the rest of your department today. Ask coworkers about their supply lists, classroom
forms, and first-day plans. Make copies of these or revise your
own work as needed. Also ask about department-wide discipline systems and procedures.

66 *I had some plans in mind for class discipline, but I wasn't quite sure how
to get started. I went next door and found other teachers on my grade level preparing discipline folders and cutting out tickets for a department-wide system
that had worked for years. All I had to do was join the group and prepare my
own folders.* **99**

Two... Allow time for a few meetings. Make as many of your first-
day copies as you can. Follow up on any textbooks or furniture
deliveries you're expecting. Then start decorating. You may
notice your classroom seems empty compared to those of other
teachers. Don't feel bad—they've been collecting decorations
for years.

One... Allow time for a few more meetings. You will probably get your tentative class list today, along with some information about what the school requires from teachers on the first day. Revise your first-day plans to includes those requirements. Arrange all planned assignments and paperwork to help your first day run smoothly. Finish making copies, if possible (the machine will be busy today). Assume that any textbooks or furniture that is not in your classroom when you leave today will not be there on Monday morning. Plan accordingly.

(Final weekend) If you weren't able to get your copies done at school, head to a copy shop so there's no room for first-day surprises. It's also possible you will want to go back to school at this point. Many schools are open the last weekend of summer for all the people who need more than ten days to complete their "ten-day" countdowns.

You won't have the totally-unprepared-teacher dream the night before school starts—that's because you won't be able to sleep until twenty minutes before your alarm clock rings. You'll probably be running on caffeine and adrenaline your first day, but to be responsible, I'll also pass on some good advice: the best thing you can do is get up early the day before school starts, exercise during the day, and wind down early so you have some chance of sleeping through the night. At least one of us has to.

Frequently Asked Questions About Starting the School Year
Q: Should I tell students this is my first time teaching?
A: No.

Q: Won't they know anyway?
A: Probably, so don't lie about it. Just add this to the long list of personal questions you try to avoid completely, which also includes

questions like "How old are you?" "Do you have a boyfriend?" and "Is that a tattoo?"

Q: I really just have one rule in my class: "Respect everyone!" Isn't that enough?

A: No! First, it's *not* your only rule. Don't you want students to come prepared? On time? Without candy and gum? Second, the word *respect* itself can be open to interpretation. Does it mean "No cursing"? "Don't interrupt"? "Don't smack your lips and curse under your breath when your teacher reminds you not to interrupt"? Respect is important in a classroom, but you will also need concrete, specific rules that are easy to enforce.

Q: My racial/cultural background is different from that of my students. Will they still listen to me?

A: There is both good and bad news for you: the good news is that great teaching crosses cultural lines. Teachers from every culture have successfully taught children from every other culture. Kids need role models who look like them, but they also need to work with and learn from people who are different. The bad news is that race and culture do make a difference. You are likely to have a few incidents that would have played out differently if you looked or sounded more like your students. No paragraph in any book will change this. Your job is to be the best teacher you can possibly be and hope the differences between you and your students fade into the background.

Q: Can I count on my class list to be accurate?

A: Most public schools are still processing new students the first week, so kids may show up who are not on your list. Plan to have space for new students and time to write down names and sign schedules. You should also know how to get more desks and think about where to seat kids if you can't get desks right away.

Q: Should I start planning on my own or wait until I meet others in my department?

A: You may be told that your department does something called collaborative planning, in which teachers meet to plan ahead, share ideas, and make sure everyone is on the same page. Though many new teachers hear of this legend, few experience it. Teachers who have taught a subject before have already made their plans. Some are possessive about the work they've put in. Others have little interest in changing their style or already work together informally. As a result, so-called collaborative planning sessions tend to be disorganized meetings that involve neither collaborating nor planning. In other cases, you may receive a curriculum or benchmark calendar during your first meeting with your department. Your plans should be flexible enough to adapt to a school calendar, but you can't go wrong planning your own first week in detail.

Q: Should I try to plan my whole year now?

A: Time is scarce during the school year, so you'll be grateful for any planning you were able to do ahead of time. Planning the entire year in detail, however, is not the best use of your time, and probably not even possible. This year will be filled with surprises that could throw off your schedule. A better idea is to start with a general sense of what students should learn this year—and when they'll have to take a big, high-stakes test to see if they've learned it. Then plan backward with this information in mind. For this, I recommend the giant, desk calendar that was on your back-to-school shopping list, but any calendar will do. Map out important dates in pen or marker. Include school holidays, state test days, and any other information that is unlikely to change. Also include progress report days and the end of each marking period so you know when grades are due (more on this in later chapters). You will use this calendar to map out academic units so they fit into the rhythm of the school year. Plan in pencil, though, and plan only your first week in detail. By the weekend, you will have an idea of how the kids act, what they can do in a day, and whether big, last-minute changes are on the horizon. Then you can block out the next plan-able chunk of time. As you feel more comfortable, you'll be able to plan further into the school year. Remember that all long-term plans should be simple overviews, not detailed, day-by-day lessons. The goal here is to avoid planning your entire year based on something that may change, but also not to be paralyzed by the fact that you can't plan everything.

Q: I still have a large pile of binders and packets that I haven't had time to look at yet. How am I going to find time to read them before school starts?

A: You're not. Find a large, cardboard box. Label it, "Ideas for Later." Keep it in your classroom closet and use it throughout the year to store potentially good materials you would like to go through when you have more time. If you're looking for a workshop packet or a unit plan donated by a generous colleague, you'll know where to find it. If you don't have the need or the time, this box can wait until winter break or even summer. Materials you will need for reference purposes, such as your district curriculum and school handbook binder, do not go in this box. Put them on a shelf near your desk so you can reach them when you need them.

Q: Should I let parents come into the room on the first day?

A: Standing up to parents the first day is hard—after all, they mean well, and you want to keep them on your side. Still, unless you teach really young children, think of a polite-but-firm response to parents who try to question you, fill you in on their children's personal problems, or inspect your room for safety hazards as they drop off their babies. This is a great gift to your students also. Kids deserve a clean slate with their peers, and Mommy coming into the room to "kiss her big, brave ninja good-bye on his first day at his new school" puts a child at a disadvantage.

Q: Should I let students help create classroom rules to show I value their opinions?

A: New teachers often receive this advice. It looks great on paper, but it's usually not worth the classroom management risk it creates. Let's face it—classroom rules are pretty standard. Students are not likely to come up with ingenious new rules on the first day; they are much more likely to make ridiculous suggestions to test you or repeat rules from past classrooms where the teacher wrote the rules anyway. Also, just because one student suggests a rule doesn't mean another will follow it. Rules seem less official when they're made up by peers. Even worse, any rule-making activity takes place, by definition, in a rule-free classroom. On the first day, you need to show that *you* are the leader in the classroom. *You* make the rules. There will be other ways to show students you value their opinions.

Q: Can I really not smile until Christmas?

A: "Don't smile until Christmas" is a sound bite of wisdom passed down through generations of teachers. It's not really about smiling. It's about breaking character and letting your guard down too early. Some teachers are strict the first week but relax the second week because the kids seem to be behaving. By the time they realize it's too soon, it's too late. This advice should really be "Don't smile—and don't let kids know you have a first name, curse, cry, like kids, want them to like you, or do anything besides eat and sleep when you're not at school—until Christmas." Just remember: the first few times you think your class is under control and it's okay to relax, you're probably wrong.

WHAT HAPPENS IF THE FIRST DAY DOESN'T GO AS PLANNED?

If your first day didn't go as planned, try to regain control tomorrow. Today, comfort yourself with the following first-day memories from experienced teachers:

"*I vividly remember my first day of teaching. I was introduced to the school and my department head by my principal. I was informed of all the wonderful activities in which students were involved. My department head was so energetic and told me she would be in my classroom the first couple of days to help me get adjusted. What I wasn't told was that my 'classroom' would be the media center. There were four other classes of thirty-five students each, sharing this one large room all day! Let's add to this madness for a minute: I had no books, and my department head didn't visit me one time my first year.***"*

—Still teaching after 10 years

"*My first day was wild. I had a book thrown at me and a student told me this was her 'f*&king' classroom.***"*

—Still teaching after 12 years

❝I had these 'community building' activities planned. The kids were supposed to fill out surveys about their favorite activities and what-not, and then we would share as a group. Well, the students were all boys who had been in the same class for years and hated each other. Several of them had documented behavior disorders. When I called on the first kid to introduce himself, other kids made fun of him before he even opened his mouth. He was a little overweight, and as soon as I read the first question—'What is your favorite activity?'—all the other boys started yelling, 'Eating!' They did this for the next few questions. I stopped the activity before we got to question number seven, 'What is your favorite food?' Needless to say, not much of a community was built.**❞**

—Still teaching after 7 years

❝I started a month into the school year, so my classes came as overload students from existing classes. It took teachers a while to send students, so in the beginning, I would psych myself up and be disappointed but also a little relieved when no one showed up. Then I got one new student. I had to make a judgment call about what to do, and I ended up teaching this kid a lesson I had planned for the entire class. Other teachers laughed at me for that one.**❞**

—Still teaching after 3 years

❝All I remember are papers flying everywhere.**❞**

—Still teaching after 14 years

❝I had come into teaching after seventeen years as an accountant. Maybe for this reason, I expected students to be sitting quietly at their desks, ready to listen to whatever I had to say. When the bell rang that first day, not one single student was sitting down. Asking them to be quiet, telling them to be quiet, even threatening them with being sent to the office all met the same response: they would close their mouths for one or two seconds, and then at the exact moment I resumed doing whatever I was doing, they started talking again. The loudest my old office got was maybe having a conversation with two people with the *dot-matrix printer running in the background. My classroom, by comparison, was like being on a runway with jets constantly taking off or landing. I couldn't think about teaching. The only thing on my mind was 'How do I get these kids to shut up?'*"

—Still teaching after 16 years

"*The first day for me was great! It led me to the irrational conclusion that the rest of my year would be as grand, but the joke was on me.*"

—Still teaching after 5 years

4

MAINTAINING AND REGAINING YOUR SANITY, ONE MONTH AT A TIME

*D*uring my first year of teaching fourth grade, I would open a cabinet, pretend I was looking for something, and silently mouth every curse word I knew. The good news was that I felt somewhat better and was able to keep from yelling curse words at my students. The bad news was I had to find something useful-looking to take out of the cabinet to keep from blowing my cover.

People constantly tell you to choose your battles in teaching. What they don't tell you is that some of the battles not worth fighting are with yourself. Being harder on yourself is not the answer to every problem. In fact, sacrificing your own happiness, sleep, and general will to live probably won't benefit your students as much as being a mentally healthy teacher who wants to be in the room with them.

You will realize that some parts of teaching make you very happy, while others make you very unhappy. You have the right to focus on the parts you love as often as possible, forgive your mistakes, and give yourself credit for what you're doing right. It's also okay to accept that some things are not under your control and to focus your efforts on the things that are. When all else fails, cursing into a cabinet works surprisingly well.

MONTH-BY-MONTH MOOD SWING CALENDAR
August/September

"*Everything is important, but not everything is equally important.***"**
>   —Abena Osei, Program Director at
>   The Breakthrough Collaborative

Up to this point, you've had the luxury of judging other teachers by what you learned in training. Now that you've jumped into the pool yourself, you realize that teaching is harder than it looks. In fact, some of the mistakes you saw experienced teachers make are completely out of your league—you won't even be able to get those details wrong until you have the big things under control. Don't be paralyzed by the belief that you need to be perfect. Just find the next thing that you need to do, and get it done.

"*I was weaned from my mentor teacher after about ten days. I was teaching with no certificate in a rough high school after having worked with college students. I actually did okay the first week, then discovered I had nothing left. I said, 'Oh! That's why we need lesson plans,' but I didn't know how to make one. I lived holiday to holiday until the second half of the year.***"**

October

"*Some days, doing 'the best we can' may still fall short of what we would like to be able to do…Doing what we can with what we have is the most we should expect of ourselves or anyone else.***"**

>   —Fred Rogers, *Mr. Rogers' Neighborhood*

This month you start to dog-paddle. You will probably have a few moments in which you feel like you've finally gotten the hang of this whole teaching thing, like it's not that hard after all, you're actually pretty good at it, maybe better than some of the other teachers in your school, absolutely incredible by any standard... followed by moments that will knock you off that ego trip so hard your tailbone stings. Let the kids who want to help you help you. Get your substitute folder in order, just in case.

❝ *On a bad day, I remind myself that, when I look back on my own experience as a student, I don't remember specific lesson plans. In the end, we remember teachers, but the individual days fade into the background. Forgive yourself for those rough days and bad lessons, and keep trying—because that's what the kids will remember.* **❞**

November

❝ *Oh, you hate your job? Maybe you can join our support group. It's called 'everybody,' and we meet at the bar.* **❞**

—Drew Carey

You became a teacher because you thought you were a certain type of person with specific things to offer your students. There will be days this month when you aren't so sure. Sometimes you will get the feeling that everything that makes you who you are has gone away and your normal personality has been replaced by this struggling, unconfident rookie desperately counting the days until Thanksgiving. If you've had a bad day recently—or even a string of bad days—you're not alone. Late October and most of November make up what the New Teacher Center calls the "disillusionment phase." This is the period in which new teachers are most likely to burst into tears in public, type up resignation letters "just in case," or fantasize about driving off a bridge on the way to work. The good news is that once you make it to Thanksgiving, you can rest over the long weekend and come back knowing there are only a few more weeks until winter break. November tests new teachers like no other month. Just remember, tests are part of the learning process.

" *Other teachers warned me November was the worst month, but I hit my own low point one day early. I was so tired I didn't realize it was Halloween and couldn't figure out why kids were bouncing off the walls. I kept punishing the class with extra homework, knowing only the good students would do it anyway. At the end of the day, another teacher asked me what fun activity I did to celebrate and I realized I was the Grinch Who Stole Every Holiday from My Students. I broke down crying in my car and had to pull into a Burger King parking lot on my way home. I still can't totally explain this, but that's okay. You won't be able to totally explain your version of this either.* **"**

December

" *You have to have a lot of patience to learn patience.* **"**

—Stanislaw J. Lec

Note to self: your students are not really demons put here to terrorize you and each other. Maintain classroom management as much as possible, but understand that you'll have to reteach procedures anyway when you come back from winter break. Use the first half of your break to rest and have some fun. Use the second half to plan for a fresh start in January. Don't be afraid to come back as the teacher you wish you had been on the first day of school. Students can forget a lot in two weeks.

❝*I was proud that I had gotten my Christmas newsletter proofed, printed, and into the kids' backpacks on time. As I was waving good-bye to the kids on the buses, my mentor teacher asked me if I had changed the letter from what I had given her to read. I told her no, it was the same one. She handed me her copy and told me to read it aloud. It was supposed to say, 'We will be making Christmas cards and placemats for the annual Christmas dinner.' What it actually said was 'We will be making Christmas cards and placentas for the annual Christmas dinner.' Moral of the story: never trust spell-check completely.*❞

January

❝*The pessimist complains about the wind; the optimist expects it to change; the realist adjusts the sails.*❞

—William Arthur Ward

Time for your new-teacher comeback! It will go about 70 percent as well as you hoped it would, but that's still enough to make it a turning point. You will still have some bad days, but those days will no longer feel like they are eighty hours long. Your school is now preparing to take the FCAT, TAKS, MCAT, GMAT, SARS, KMART, or whatever multiple-choice test is supposed to prove you are teaching the curriculum using fabulous lessons that appeal to all learning styles. Don't panic if you haven't been marinating your students in test prep the whole year, but do make the most of this month to get them ready for any tests they have to take.

❝*Learning to teach is like furnishing a house. When you first start, things seem pretty bare, but you keep finding new things that will work with your style and adding to what you have. You are never completely done. There are always a few details you can improve.*❞

February

❝ *You just can't beat the person who never gives up.* **❞**

—Babe Ruth

"The Test" is coming, either this month or early next month. Get ready to see the worst side of everyone, including you. You will at some point feel like killing yourself as you go over practice exams with your students. Don't worry. They feel like killing you too.

❝ *Our school put up handmade posters everywhere, saying things like 'Do your best! Beat that test!' Everyone talked about it every day. The teachers had to wear shirts on Mondays that said, 'Wake up! It's test time!' I was scrambling to do as much last-minute review as possible, but deep down I didn't think my kids were going to do very well. I felt guilty about cranking up the pressure when they weren't prepared. I also worried I wouldn't be rehired if they did poorly.* **❞**

March

❝ *Good judgment comes from experience. And experience, well, that comes from bad judgment.* **❞**

—Unknown

Okay, I didn't want to tell you this earlier, but your friends are sick of hearing you talk about your students. It is time to remember you are still a person, not only a teacher.

❝ *I got to a point where I related everything in my life to teaching. I talked about 'differentiating' my laundry and 'staying on task' at the gym. One day I started describing my man problems to my roommate using classroom management terms—something about how I should have set and modeled* *expectations and enforced consequences consistently. I realized midsentence that I sounded psycho.* 99

April

66 *Only those who have learned a lot are in a position to admit how little they know.* 99

—L. Carte

You will realize it is April already, and that's a good feeling. If you have made it this far, you'll make it through your first year just fine. Every now and then, you feel guilty that this year has been such a "learning experience." There are so many things you wish you had handled differently, but now you want to put most of your energy toward next year's kids—the ones you haven't made mistakes with yet. Like that stupid cat poster says, "Hang in there!!!" In addition to your now very full "Ideas for Later" box, you'll want to start a more specific list of things you'd like to do next year.

66 *Near the end of the year, I finally found ways to help some of my struggling students. I should have been happy, but instead I was mad at myself for not figuring it out earlier.* 99

May/June

66 *There will come a time when you believe everything is finished. That will be the beginning.* 99

—Louis L'Amour

You can begin a daily countdown now—unless, of course, you've been counting down since January. Yes, you are tired, but take some time to enjoy your kids now that you know each other. Look for ideas to keep you from going through the last month of school on autopilot. On the very last days, get students to help you clean, organize, and pack up for next year. They love doing it, and you will love the help because this is a big job.

" *Looking back, I realize I actually enjoyed parts of my first year. I remember that class the way people remember their first loves: it wasn't always easy, but I can still picture the good times. Sometimes I look back and think, 'If only I had known then what I know now.' Those were the kids who taught me. Even so, on their last day of school, all I wanted was for them to leave so I could go home and sleep.* **"**

5

PILES AND FILES: ORGANIZATION AND TIME MANAGEMENT

I've been to one workshop on classroom organization. I signed up when I realized I would not be successful using my initial system, which was collecting paperwork in one giant pile, then cramming it into an accordion folder to separate into smaller piles at home.

The main thing I learned at the workshop was that some people really enjoy organizing things, and anyone who gives training sessions on how to stay organized is way out of my league. From what I remember, the presentation sounded something like this:

Since your class will already be divided into teams, each team should have a separate color. Whenever you ask students to do something, give five points to the first team to finish, four to the second team, and so on, until everyone is following directions. Be sure to use color-coded chalk to mark down the points. At the end of the day, all you have to do is write down how many points each team has earned in the children's folders. Then keep track of those points during the week. On Fridays you add up the total points for the year on a chart...I like to have a hanging file folder for each student and a computerized list with each child's basic information, plus home language, since I speak three languages, and also their birth order. In fact, I recommend you keep a book about birth order behind your desk in your "Child Psychology Book" file... When you color-code your...bla bla bla...You probably already have index cards with all the information about... And if you don't have extra copies of...It would just be irresponsible not to be able to show parents that you have everything dated and typed when you...Sometimes you will want to organize your data by student ID, but other times you will want to arrange things by...It is best to have a different colored file for each...bla bla bla... spreadsheet...bla bla bla...laminate...bla bla bla...plastic sheet protectors...just to make your life easier.

I slumped farther down in my chair every time I heard the words *color-coded* or *of course you have already*. By the end of the presentation, only my neck and shoulders were touching the seat. I was no more organized, but I was fully convinced I had no business being a teacher—or maybe even alive—at my current organizational level.

The only thing that made me feel better was that the presenter forgot to give out the required evaluation at the end of the session. This meant that (1) she had to track down everyone to send us evaluation forms and (2) maybe her organization system wasn't so perfect after all.

I never did start using plastic sheet protectors, but over time I was able to replace my "Things to Do Soon" folder with a decent filing system. I am proud to announce my desk no longer looks like I am building a fort. However, if someone had given me the following lists before my first year, I would have saved many trips to Office Depot. These lists won't be perfect, but they'll give you a starting point you can adjust to fit your needs. You can color-code them if you want to.

LOW-MAINTENANCE FILES FOR ALMOST ANY PAPER THAT TOUCHES YOUR DESK

(Keep within reaching distance and handwrite all labels.)

Hanging Folder Labels	Inner Folder Labels	What Goes Inside
Period ___ class forms (you will need one of these folders for each class you teach)	Blank Forms	• Extra copies of any blank forms you have created for this class (grade sheets, sign-in sheets, etc.)
	Completed Forms	• Class lists with student information • Class lists with student signatures • Textbook lists • Grade printouts from computerized grading systems
Grade-Level or Department Information		• Papers from grade-level or department meetings
Employment	Certification	• Papers given only to first-year teachers • Paperwork or evaluations from training programs • Extra copies of certification coursework
	General Employment	• Evaluations from your principal • A copy of your contract • Union information

Hanging Folder Labels	Inner Folder Labels	What Goes Inside
Employment *(cont'd)*	Substitute Teacher	• Information on how to get a substitute (also keep a copy of this at home)
Emergency		• Emergency information you don't need to post on your wall
End of the Year		• Papers you receive the first week but probably won't need until the end of the year (inventory sheets, etc.)
Pull Later		• Papers you're not sure you need but are afraid to throw out
New Students		• Extra copies of papers you gave out on the first day (stapled into packets if possible)
Documentation	Forms Turned in to Office	• Dated copies of paperwork turned in to the office, to the school district, or to anyone in your school who may lose it
	Comments	• Positive notes from students, parents, or administrators • Documentation of unfairness, paranoia, anger-management issues, etc., for anyone who is making your life hard for no reason
Blank Teacher-Made Forms (with no student names)	Lesson Plans	• Extra copies of a blank lesson plan sheet, even if you usually type lesson plans
	Student Signatures	• Extra copies of blank forms for student signatures
	Checklists	• Extra copies of a blank, all-purpose checklist
	Seating Charts	• Extra copies of a blank seating chart that matches your classroom layout

Hanging Folder Labels	Inner Folder Labels	What Goes Inside
Blank Teacher-Made Forms (with no student names) *(cont'd)*	Parent Contact Logs	• Enough blank parent contact logs for each student in your class
Blank School Forms	As Needed	• Failure notices • Schoolwide hall passes • Honors/gifted recommendation forms • Debt slips • Copy forms • Attendance correction slips • Progress reports • Grade book pages • Maintenance • Etc.
Stickers		• Stickers
Discipline	As Needed	• At least ten copies each of discipline forms supplied by your school (detention forms, referrals, etc.) • Forms you have created for discipline purposes
Sample Student Work		• Outstanding student work for future examples
Teacher Aides		• Lists of duties your assistants can help with and directions if necessary • Community-service-hour forms for teacher aides
Testing		• Testing schedules for school wide tests • Test proctoring materials
(Extra folders)	(Extra manila folders)	• New folders for anything that does not fit in the above files

STACKABLE TRAYS FOR INCOMING PAPERS

(Keep these on or next to your desk.)

Tray Title	What Goes Inside
In-Box	All paperwork you actually need to handle. (Some of what you get in your office mailbox should be reviewed and thrown out immediately.)
Grade	Student work you plan to grade and record in your grade book (divided into folders by period if applicable).
"Middle" File	Student work that was just for practice and that you plan to throw out in a reasonable amount of time if no one has asked for it. (This is like a secret garbage can behind your desk that will save you the trouble of sorting through a three-inch pile of papers later. Label it with a vague yet important-sounding name.)
Pass Back/File	Graded work that needs to be filed or passed back to students (divided into folders by period if applicable).
Parent Contact	Records folders of students whose parents you need to call.

TWO TYPES OF STUDENT FOLDERS

(These make your life easier but are time-consuming to create.
Look for helpers to label folders and set up files.)

Folder	Description
Student Work	Many districts require a portfolio of graded student work. Divide these into file boxes by either class period or last name. Students should file their own papers after looking at them, or helpers can file the papers and students can check them at a convenient time.

Folder	Description
Student Records	These should stay behind your desk or in a locked drawer. They contain contact information and documentation for each student. Tape the information sheets from the first day of school to the front of each folder. The first time you contact a parent, tape a contact log to the inside flap and document the conversation. Put other paperwork into the folder as needed. If you need to contact a parent, put this folder in your parent contact in-box so you will have both contact info and records of past conversations at your fingertips. Then refile it after the conversation. Later, you can pull these folders and walk into parent conferences with confidence.

LEFTOVER COPIES FROM PAST LESSONS

In our constant fear of being one copy short, teachers often make a few extras of every worksheet. It is tempting to stack these in too-soon-to-throw-it-out piles until they cover every surface and climb our classroom walls like a game of Tetris. A better habit is to put extras of any paper in a labeled manila folder. Put these into a box or file drawer as soon as possible. Folders don't need to be perfectly organized, but they should stay with other assignments on the same topic. Unless you need copies for a student who was absent, you can ignore these folders and organize them better when you have more time.

STUDENT RESPONSIBILITY: AN OXYMORON?

No. Students should be responsible for keeping track of their own work. How responsible, and for how much work? This depends on what you can reasonably expect from your students and from yourself.

One teacher I know has each student number the pages of a spiral notebook at the beginning of the semester. The students use the notebook to take notes and tape their graded work into it as the year goes on so that everyone is—literally—on the same page. This requires the teacher to provide a sample notebook for absent students, schedule frequent notebook checks, leave the correct number of blank pages for graded work, and consistently hand back work in time to go on the appropriate page. If you like the thought of managing this type of system, you, too, can teach your students valuable organization skills. If you would rather eat a big plate of your own hair, look for a system that takes less maintenance.

As you decide how students should keep track of their work, consider the likely answers to the following multiple-choice questions:

1. Can you reasonably expect students to bring notebooks every day?

    a. Yes, and I will have consequences for those who are unprepared.

    b. Yes, and I plan to run my class as if every student had a notebook. If they choose to carry their class notes folded up in their pockets, it will be their grades that suffer.

    c. No, but my students will keep all materials in their desks.

    d. No, but I have a specific place in the classroom to keep notebooks. Students will get them as they walk in, or a student helper will be responsible for distributing and collecting them.

2. How do you plan to handle filing of student work?

    a. Student helpers will file graded work. Kids will have a specific time when they are allowed to check their files, but no more than one-fourth of the class will be near file boxes at a time. Some students won't bother to check their folders unless I remind them, but this doesn't bother me. In fact, I'm kind of happy about it.

b. I will pass out graded work and expect students to file it after they look at it. Work will go in file boxes or in folders I distribute. In some cases, I will pass back several assignments at once while students are working. No more than one-fourth of the class will be near file boxes at a time.

c. Once work is filed, I will tell the whole class to check their folders at the same time. Whoever pushes hardest will get to see their grades first. I am willing to break up file-related fights.

d. I don't want students to do any filing. I am willing to add this to my other job responsibilities in the interest of student privacy.

3. Do you expect parents to see or sign graded work?

a. Yes. I will send graded work or progress reports to parents on a specific day each week. I will have enough time or responsible helpers to get this done consistently, and I will implement rewards and consequences to make sure folders come back signed. I am willing to act against or ignore forged signatures.

b. Yes. I will send graded work or progress reports home periodically. I will have students sign a list to prove they took these papers home. If parents come to complain about a grade, I will have documentation that students were aware of their progress.

c. No. I am not going to spend class time checking signatures that many students will forge anyway. I will follow school procedures regarding progress reports and have students sign a list proving they received their grades.

d. No. I will leave it to students to communicate grades to parents. I understand this means most parents will have no clue how their kids are doing in my class.

4. Which of these is most important to you when students put away papers and materials?

a. I want it done as quietly as possible even if it takes a little more time. I plan to enforce noise-level rules while students put away supplies.

b. I want it done as quickly as possible even if it gets noisy. I plan to put a time limit on cleanup or to reward the first students ready for the next activity.

c. I want things put away in the right place every time. I am willing to take extra time to inspect students' desks or notebooks, and let more organized kids help their classmates.

d. I would like students to crumple their used papers into basketballs or leave them on the floor for me to clean up.

5. How do you feel about thirty children opening and closing their binder rings AS LOUDLY AS THEY POSSIBLY CAN?

a. I would love to teach a lesson while my students start a binder-loudness contest.

b. I can deal with the noise as long as it happens only at appropriate times.

c. It will drive me nuts. I will teach students to close their binders like normal people and enforce a "quiet binder" policy as needed.

d. Forget it. We'll use folders or notebooks.

TIME MANAGEMENT AT SCHOOL

Time and space are connected. After creating files to keep papers from collecting on your desk, you need to schedule slots of time to keep papers from collecting in your files. If not, you will place yourself on the "Oh, s#*t!!!" time-management plan, in which work divides itself into two categories: things that can wait until tomorrow and things that (Oh, s#*t!) can't. When you make your weekly schedule, plan specific times for each of the following responsibilities:

- Grading and recording grades.
- Parent contact. (Take the folders out of your parent contact tray and document the conversation before refiling them.)
- District paperwork.
- Lesson planning.
- Extracurricular activities (if applicable).
- Certification forms and coursework.

General Time-Management Tips

- **Handle small tasks immediately.** Don't stick something in your in-box if you can handle it in less than five minutes. Some incoming papers only need signatures. Others can go directly into a file or recycling bin.
- **Save your energy for what's important.** Rush through district surveys and senseless busywork as quickly as possible. Spend most of your effort on work that truly affects your teaching.
- **Sign up for direct deposit and automatic bill pay.** The last thing you will want to do after finishing school paperwork is come home to more paperwork.
- **Plan time to do things you enjoy.** You are not a robot. A schedule that never gives you time for yourself will be difficult to stick with.

- **Follow the work habit advice you give to your students.** Stop playing with your phone. No, this is not group work. Finish your work now or you'll have to take it home for homework, and that is no guarantee you will get it done. When you do take work home, be realistic about how much time you will have to work on it. Then plan accordingly, so you can come to class prepared.

6
YOUR TEACHER PERSONALITY: FAKING IT, MAKING IT

*W*hy does it seem so easy for kids to spot new teachers? Is it the excitement in our voices? The idealistic gleam in our eyes? The way our hands shake as we try to unlock our classroom doors with what turns out to be our car keys? Even though we know not to share our first-year status with students, we sometimes feel like imposters in loose-fitting teacher Halloween costumes. We are sure it's only a matter of time before someone blows our cover and screams, "Hey, you're not a real teacher!"

It takes a while to develop a convincing teacher personality. Some people will tell you just to be yourself in the classroom, but be careful. This advice should never be taken literally. For both your students' sake and your own, the person you are on the weekend should be different from the teacher who walks in Monday morning.

They shouldn't be opposites, though. Teaching is a shift from your first-name self to your last-name self, not a complete character overhaul. Like your work clothes, your teacher personality should be a professional twist on your current style.

One common rookie mistake is trying to copy the classroom

persona of a master teacher, especially one who is very different from you. You can learn a lot from other teachers, but adopting someone else's personality is as hard in teaching as it would be in your everyday life. Another thing to keep in mind is that weaknesses in your personal life will probably carry over to your teaching. If "Dan Martin" has a stack of unpaid bills and parking tickets, "Mr. Martin" is likely to have a pile of ungraded papers. Promising a two-day turnaround on student work will probably backfire. If "Yolanda Jones" is not a morning person, "Ms. Jones" shouldn't plan to start the day with a happy class song. Your goal is not to conceal your weaknesses or disguise them as strengths. It is to identify your true strengths and use them to reinforce potential weak spots.

Your best bet is to start the year serious, mature, and focused on your subject matter. As you get to know your students, channel the parts of yourself that naturally help you teach them. Look for role models who share your strengths and can help you build your style around them.

WHAT ARE YOUR STRENGTHS?

Use the following list to figure out which of these assets come naturally to you and put them to work immediately. Keep in mind that some of these traits contradict each other and that no one has them all.

Patience and understanding A teacher who listens to students and gets to know them as individuals will motivate them from the inside out. The true benefits of being a patient teacher will emerge as the year goes on, after you have had a chance to win over one student at a time.

Perseverance Maybe it's a matter of pride. Maybe you're just stubborn. In teaching, it won't matter why you hang on so tightly. What matters is once you start something, you see it through, and your students need someone who won't give up on them.

Knowledge of your subject matter   Whether you're bringing skills from a former career or just really know your stuff, kids are lucky to have a teacher who's an expert in the field.

Knowledge of the neighborhood   If you're working in your own neighborhood or one like it, you get to skip a whole layer of culture shock that other teachers may experience. If you live in the area, you may even know some of your students' families—a big advantage when you need to call home.

Sense of humor   You don't want to whip out the jokes too soon, but gradually you can let kids notice your ability to make them laugh. A person who can make students laugh without getting off the subject is a person who can make them listen, and a person who can make kids listen is a person who can make them learn.

Organization   Kids need structure. They even like it once they get it. You need and like structure even more. Organized teachers have an easier time being consistent and following through on consequences, which means better discipline with less yelling. You will also know how to manage the new demands on your time and the papers on your desk.

Large size   You know you would never put your hands on a student. However, students tend to listen more quickly to teachers who could physically crush them.

Loud, authoritative voice   Even though you shouldn't be yelling all the time, a voice that sounds like you mean business gives you an edge in classroom management.

Energy   Kids are notorious for wearing out adults with their hyperactive ways. Being a little hyper yourself helps you keep up.

Good people skills   People like you. Kids are people. If your students like you as a person, they're more likely to do what you say just because it's you who said it.

Work ethic   You show up every day. You come early. You get things done on schedule and do them right the first time, even if you could get away with less. Not only will this make you an all-around better teacher, but it also sets a great example for the kids.

Stage presence   When you talk, people listen. If your natural charisma holds your students' attention, they'll disrupt less and learn more.

Confidence   Believing in yourself works for you in two ways. First, it shows through in your actions and helps you establish yourself as a leader. Second, it keeps you from taking the bad days personally.

Character   Even when no one's watching, you stick to your principles because being a good person is important to you. Part of our job as teachers is raising students to be the people we want sharing our world. Kids notice when you practice the values you preach.

Creativity and problem-solving skills   A creative teacher is more likely to keep class interesting and inspire creativity from students. A creative mind will also help you deal with the many situations that were not addressed in training. Teaching can test you in ways that are clearly "outside the box."

Ability to stay calm and think clearly under stress   If you can juggle many things at once without going crazy, you'll cope better with those moments in teaching where you need to, well, juggle many things at once without going crazy.

Bossy attitude   As the teacher, you are the boss. If you have some bossy tendencies to begin with, you are more likely to slide into this role comfortably.

Kids of your own What is a teacher if not a part-time parent with thirty children? It should be no surprise that many parenting skills transfer well to teaching.

Ambition A results-oriented person will focus on pushing kids to their limits, which often translates to greater achievement, and—to your principal's delight—higher test scores.

Positive attitude and a passion for teaching If you're excited about being in the classroom, the kids will know, and they'll be more excited to be there with you.

Case Study 1: Good at Setting Up, Bad at Keeping Up

“*I'm great at thinking up imaginative classroom systems, but I don't keep up with everyday details very well. This caught up with me when I started a 'compliment chain' for my second-graders. The idea was to add one paper loop every time the kids received a compliment, then have a pizza party when the chain reached across the room. Unfortunately, it never did. It was too high on the wall for the kids to add loops, so I had to set aside time to climb on a desk after school. I never quite got around to it. After two months, the chain only had about five loops, and my students figured out there would be no pizza party. This experience taught me that for a system to succeed, my kids must be able to manage it on their own. I was eventually able to make the compliment reward work by combining it with an existing system for recess time. Every time an adult commented on their good behavior, a student helper added a minute to the class's recess board. The kids were happy with the more immediate payoff. I was happy to throw out the depressingly short 'compliment chain.'***”**

Case Study 2: Bad at Keeping Order, Good at Pushing Forward

“*I'm not a loud person, and classroom management has never been my strong suit. What works for me is setting ambitious goals for student achievement and***

monitoring kids' progress throughout the year. I hand back graded work every day and chart students' progress toward their goals. Students know someone is watching what they do on an individual level, which makes them take their work more seriously. My kids still talk more than I want them to, but they get their work done. Last year, my classes won two of the top three spots in a schoolwide reading contest. They even beat some quieter classes, which made me feel I must be doing something right. **"**

Case Study 3: You.

What are the strengths you believe you bring to teaching? What are the weaknesses you worry may undermine you? The more realistic you are in answering these questions, the more quickly you will develop a teaching style that rests on your strengths.

"FAKE IT TILL YOU MAKE IT"
Tips for Looking Less Like a Rookie

There's no guarantee that the kids will think you've taught before, but the following tips will help you seem more prepared and experienced. They will also make you an all-around better teacher, regardless of your teaching style.

1. **Set a tone of decency.** Start the day by saying "Good morning" to your students and expect them to say it back. Say "Bless you" when someone sneezes. These simple routines teach manners and show you care. Students will pick up your habits.

2. **Set an example of seriousness.** Get to school before your students do. Have materials laid out in advance when possible. Keep your cell phone silent, your private life private, and your language school-appropriate. These actions show you mean it when you say class time is for class activities.

3. **Prepare to show you care**. Keep Band-Aids in your desk drawer and have hand sanitizer and tissues in an accessible place.

Secondary teachers can stock supplies for feminine emergencies. You may also want to buy packages of blank cards to use for birthday, sympathy, or get-well wishes. Pass these around as needed so that every student can sign.

4. **Encourage students to learn one another's names**. Team-building activities on the first day are risky, but kids should grow to be on a first-name basis if you want them to see class as a community. You don't want students to spend the year referring to one another as "the short kid in the back" or "that girl with the lazy eye."

5. **Respect student privacy.** Never bring up anything about a student's medical, academic, psychological, or family history in front of other students. Keep kids' special-ed, ESL, and free-lunch status a secret. Always give students a chance to keep their writing personal, and ask before you use student work as an example. Don't read grades out loud, and use discretion when asking students to peer-edit or file graded work. Showing you can keep a lid on personal info takes you a long way toward gaining kids' trust.

6. **Polish your teacher look.** Of course you've already heard of the teacher look, that one-second glance that taps the brakes on bad behavior. Now you need one that fits you. To find your natural teacher look, imagine you are at a store with your grandmother and she is waiting for her change. The snotty teenage cashier takes his time and even turns around for a full five minutes to talk to a friend at another register before whipping out his cell phone and sending a text message. Then, instead of handing your grandmother the six dollars he owes her, he puts the money in a jar labeled "Tips for Excellent Service." Now freeze! Look in the mirror. That, my friend, is your teacher look. Practice holding it for as long as necessary. If you are

tempted to break character, pull up a preselected memory of an event that made you feel ready to jump out of your seat and choke someone. That feeling—and that readiness—is the driving force behind a successful teacher look.

7. **Line up your teacher lines.** Remember those old-fashioned phrases from your own teachers that you promised would never come out of your mouth? Teachers don't always have time to think of original comebacks, but experienced educators have a supply of preloaded comments for common situations. If you don't want to fall back on clichés from your own teachers, get some quick lines ready for students who nag, complain about boredom, or ask you personal questions when they should be working. Otherwise you may be shocked when, in a desperate moment, you hear yourself yelling, "I'm not just doing this for my health, people!"

7

CLASSROOM MANAGEMENT: EASIER SAID THAN DONE

PHASE I
Trying to Do It by the Book

Classroom management is a series of straightforward rules tested by millions of teachers and proven to work: clearly lay out rules and procedures in advance. Have a specific chain of consequences for misbehavior. And give positive reinforcement for following rules. Create a classroom culture in which students respect each other and *want* to learn. Of course, as any teacher can tell you, planning engaging lessons has a lot to do with this. Most important, be consistent.

Well, you knew all this. In fact, you spent a *long* time making a "star chart" with each child's name on a star and explaining, "We are all stars in this classroom!" You informed your students that they had the chance to become "shining stars," or even "superstars" by behaving well. Unfortunately, they could also end up as "falling stars" if they didn't follow the rules, which were printed in positive language on a large poster at the front of the classroom.

To make sure your expectations were clear, you asked a volunteer to demonstrate sitting quietly and waiting his turn. "Very good!" you said.

Then, to be even clearer, you let a student act out what it meant to be a "bad kid." This kid did a perfect impression. He got out of his seat, insulted another student, and threw paper on the floor. He talked in what can only be described as an "outdoor voice." He had the class laughing and was definitely enjoying the attention. The only problem is, now you can't get him to stop and the class is still laughing. An hour later, he has worked through your chain of clearly stated consequences like Pac-Man but still won't raise his hand to talk. You have silently nicknamed him "Consequence King." His best friend is showing all the signs of becoming "Consequence Prince."

After lunch, the clock moves much more slowly than your students do. Your class begins to remind you of a bar full of little drunk people: they want constant attention and often don't realize how loud they are talking. They have short attention spans, rarely think of the consequences of their actions, and, as you will find out tomorrow, they don't always remember what happened the day before.

At the end of the day, no one's name has moved up to "shining star," let alone "superstar." This is because you spent the whole day trying to keep Consequence King and his two (now three) new followers from starting an open-participation-anonymous-fart-sound contest. To make matters worse, your memory of the chaos includes a flurry of desperation moves that can only be described as inconsistent: you threatened to call everyone's parents. You yelled at only one student when at least five were talking. You might have mentioned something about a pizza party. Panic slices through your exhaustion.

You describe the situation to another teacher, whose relaxed attitude shows that her day did not include any of these problems.

"Oh, sweetie, it's easy. What you *should have done* is clearly lay out your rules and consequences, give positive reinforcement, make sure your lesson plans are…" You stop listening for a minute here because you just realized how much your feet hurt. Anyway, you know what she's going to end with, don't you? "…Above all, *be consistent.*"

Well-Known Classroom Management Advice and How to Make It Happen

If advice and intentions were enough, we would all floss, call our grandmothers every week, and get our oil changed every three months or 3,000 miles. We would keep our New Year's resolutions, and we would certainly follow the classroom management principles we learned in training. Unfortunately, most management sound bites are easier said than done. Some setbacks are due to outside circumstances. Others are caused by our own inexperience. Either way, we don't need to hear the same advice repeated. We're looking for an answer to our real questions: "Why isn't this working?" and "How can I make it work?"

ADVICE
Be consistent.
Why It Helps

- **Kids have super-sharp "fairness" radar.** Threats and promises work best when they are backed up by action and when rules apply to everyone.
- **Good kids want to see you know who's causing the problem.** That's because it isn't them.
- **The "bad kids" need to see someone else get the punishment they got yesterday.** That way they know you weren't just picking on them.
- **Some kids will test rules more than once.** Repeat offenders need extra proof that you mean business.

Why It's Easier Said Than Done

- **Students don't have consistent needs.** One student sometimes takes as much of your attention as the rest of the class put together, and you might have more than one of these students in a class. You may have students with behavioral disorders who have trouble controlling themselves. It's hard to know if you should hold them to the same standard.

- **Students don't have consistent behavior.** Some kids are so much better behaved than others that you want to let them slide on the first offense. At the same time, you don't want to seem like you are favoring anyone. Sometimes you're tempted to come down on a good kid to show the troublemakers it's not just them. There are also kids who get on your nerves. You may blame them for problems too often or overcompensate by ignoring their bad behavior.

- **Let's be honest—sometimes you don't feel so consistent yourself.** It's hard to be fair when you are tired and a million things are happening at once. You can't respond to everything you see, and you don't see everything that happens.

How to Make It Easier to Do

- **Promise less.** When possible, don't promise or threaten to call home—just do it. If you can't get to it that night or the number doesn't work, at least you kept your mouth shut and didn't lose credibility.

- **Look the other way.** If an offense is not serious and you can't deal with it right away, pretend you didn't see it. If the kids think you didn't notice, you're not being inconsistent. They'll just think someone got away with something.

- **Follow through—reasonably.** Instead of telling students you will do something every week or by a certain day, do things as often or as soon as you *can*. This includes things like changing seats or updating in-class progress reports. The more you follow a routine, the more you will get your students into a routine, but if you promise to establish a routine you can't keep up with, kids are less likely to buy into your next idea.

- **Turn follow-up plans into classroom jobs**. Kids enjoy being helpful, and an enthusiastic student can run some systems *better* than an overwhelmed teacher. Whenever possible, let students update charts and files and remember everyday tasks. You can even give certain jobs as rewards for the students who remind you they need to be done each day.

- **Get as much sleep as possible.** Well-rested people are more alert and better prepared to react to surprises. They are also less likely to overreact to small frustrations (aka children).

- **When in doubt, be too strict.** It is always easier to relax your enforcement of a rule than to enforce it after you've been letting it slide.

ADVICE
Teaching routines and procedures will help stop problems before they start.
Why It Helps

- **Procedures set a starting point.** When most students are doing the right thing most of the time, you are free to focus on trouble spots.

- **The fewer students out of their seats, the better.** Students are more likely to get loud and foolish when they're not sure what else to do. By planning the way you use time and space in your classroom, you can eliminate many opportunities to cause trouble.

Why It's Easier Said Than Done

- **Recognizing trouble spots comes with experience.** Some systems that look good on paper don't work the way you thought they would.

- **Teachers contradict each other.** Every teacher has different routines. Some teachers want books put away fast. Others want things done quietly, or everything laid out in a specific order. The habits students picked up from their past teachers may drive you crazy.

- **Kids have short memories—and so do you.** Kids forget the details of your routines unless you constantly reinforce them. You may forget schoolwide procedures that you didn't make up yourself. In fact, there are some procedures you'll forget even though you did make them up.

How to Make It Easier to Do

- **Keep procedures as simple and natural as possible.** Routines fall flat if they're awkward for students—or for you. If you won't feel comfortable saying, "One, two, three, all eyes on me!" every time you want kids to be quiet, don't make that the signal for their attention. There is nothing wrong with just saying, "I need your attention," or, "Okay, look up here." In some cases, things also flow more naturally if you build in a bit of lead time by saying, "Be ready to listen in thirty seconds…twenty…ten…" This gives students a chance to finish their explanations or questions before immediately snapping to attention. It also avoids drawing kids into a power struggle about how fast you can get them to be quiet.

- **Practice.** Walk students through routines many times so they remember them.

- **Build on systems that work.** Once you find a solid plan, like assigning numbers to students in line, use it as a foundation for other procedures. Can you use those numbers to divide students into teams, call on them to answer questions, or assign class jobs?

- **Adjust systems that need fixing.** It's tempting to overhaul your procedures every time you think of a new idea, but this gets confusing. If a routine isn't working, figure out why. It may be hard to remember, too complicated, or inappropriate for the age group you teach. Some routines just need minor changes that you can phase in gradually.

- **Get rid of systems that are bad beyond repair.** Some ideas don't need adjustments—they need to go. When I switched from fourth grade to high school, I spent half a period trying to get my first class to give me the "thumbs up, thumbs down" signal to show they understood the lesson. They all just looked at me like I was out of my mind.

ADVICE
Establish clear rules and consequences.
Why It Helps

- **Your rules keep you on track so you can keep students on track.** Having a big poster gives you a reference point to deal with misbehavior.
- **Letting students know what you expect is only fair.** Students will know when they've crossed a line if you've drawn clear lines from the beginning. If you haven't, they won't.

Why It's Easier Said Than Done

- **The rules poster itself means very little to students.** Your rules poster is for you, your principal, and your students—in that order. The only real rules in your classroom are the ones you consistently enforce, which brings us back to all the challenges of being consistent.
- **Rules change.** You don't always know at the beginning of your first year what rules are going to work for you. Some rules are broken so often it's hard to give consequences every time.
- **Your chain of consequences won't work the same for every student.** Calling home, for example, is only as much of a consequence as parents make it. In addition, consequences take time both during and after class.
- **You don't want to write too many referrals.** The most serious consequences involve school administration, and, as a new teacher, you are working to establish your own reputation. You don't want administrators to question your management ability or stop taking

your problems seriously. This is assuming your administrators even handle discipline referrals effectively—at some schools, sending a student to the office means next to nothing.

How to Make It Easier to Do

- **Set rules that stop behavior before it gets on your nerves.** If you don't want kindergartners pushing in line, the rule to enforce is "arms folded." If you don't want high school students using cell phones, your rule should be "If I see a phone, I will take it for the rest of the day." This will keep you from having to argue about whether a student was sending a text message or "just checking the time."

- **Look for simple solutions.** If time on the class computer makes your students happy, you may not need store-bought prizes or elaborate point systems. Making troublemakers work solo during group activities can be more effective than calling home after school. A reward is anything you can convince kids to work for, and a consequence is anything they find unpleasant.

- **Don't post your consequences on the wall.** Training courses often tell teachers to display a step-by-step chain of consequences next to their rules poster, but this can backfire. While your consequences should be well thought-out and relatively consistent, you also want to leave yourself some flexibility in case you want to switch from individual to group consequences. Posting a chain of consequences also lets students know your enforcement options are limited. It can be more effective to let kids use their imagination than to point out that they have already passed step one, "verbal warning," and are now headed toward step two, "name on the board." Oooooooh, scary.

- **Use peer pressure.** A student who won't stop whispering for you might stop for thirty classmates who want to keep their recess time or who don't want a pop quiz on last night's history homework.

- **Be open to change.** If a rule is broken too often to enforce consequences, think about whether it's one of the battles you want to choose. Is it so terrible if kids write in colored ink? Do you really care if your ESL students keep calling you "Miss" or "Mister" instead of using your full name? If you realize a rule is less important than you thought, change it. Better yet, stop enforcing it and students will forget it ever existed.

- **Remember: it's your classroom.** You can change or add rules in the middle of the year if you need to. Students may whine, grumble, or challenge you at first, but, if you explain your reasons and stick with the change, they'll get used to it.

- **Keep pushing for better behavior.** If every student followed every rule every day, you wouldn't need that big poster in the first place. A well-run classroom is a process, not a starting point. Keep reaching for that goal even if you lose ground some days.

ADVICE
Give positive reinforcement when kids do things right.
Why It Helps

- **It makes kids happy.** We all like to be recognized when we do something well.

- **Students want your attention.** Positive reinforcement shows them they can get it without misbehaving.

Why It's Easier Said Than Done

- **It doesn't always make sense.** If one kid is doing something horrible, it's awkward to ignore the situation and praise a good student for basic social skills.

- **It can backfire.** Some students see positive reinforcement as "reverse psychology" and find it corny or insulting. In addition, making an example out of good kids could set them up as targets for bullies.

How to Make It Easier to Do

- **Compliment or reward a whole group.** When you compliment a group of students, you avoid singling out a kid who might be shy. Groups know who got them a reward, just as they know who got them in trouble when you punish them.

- **Praise shy students discreetly.** You can compliment kids privately by writing comments on their work or by anonymously using their ideas as examples for the class. You can say, "One of my students organized the assignment this way and it came out great." Students will recognize their ideas even if you don't mention names.

- **Tone it down a little.** If you find students rolling their eyes when you praise them, your compliments may sound forced. Nodding and saying "Not bad" can be more effective than a whole cheerleading routine, especially for older or more cynical students. Staying low-key also makes it more meaningful when you do pull out the pom-poms.

ADVICE
A well-planned, engaging lesson will solve most behavior problems.
Why It Helps

- **Good lessons keep kids focused on learning.** This means they have less time to focus on making other kids cry.

Why It's Easier Said Than Done

- **Kids are at different levels.** What seems engaging to one student may bore or overwhelm another.

- **This so-called common sense advice is not always true.** In reality, making kids do worksheets all day will solve most behavior problems. That's why teachers who don't want to be bothered dealing with children—which includes dealing with childlike behavior— pass out packets and then sit at their own desks. A hands-on, interesting activity that you spent time on, especially one that involves scissors and glue (and *National Geographic* magazines), actually creates *more* chances for kids to act up. It also creates more opportunities for them to learn, though, and you didn't become a teacher to sit at your desk while students do busywork.

How to Make It Easier to Do

- **Think ahead.** Talk through your most active lessons with a teacher who can help you troubleshoot without shooting down your ideas.
- **Make expectations clear.** Time everything. Check or collect all work. Discuss student behavior before any new activity. Don't assume students already know how to act. They will probably prove you wrong.
- **Plan some silent time into your day.** Have a few set, quiet activities that keep kids busy and happy if they finish early. These can include drawing, review activities, or reading. Also be prepared to shut down fun group activities and have kids do silent, individual work instead. Students need to know they share responsibility for making fun activities run smoothly.

ADVICE
You need to build a supportive classroom culture that encourages respect, personal responsibility, hard work, and achievement (like I do).

Why It Helps

- **It's true.** This is another way of saying that being a wonderful teacher will make your class better. Who can argue with that?

Why It's Easier Said Than Done

- **It's useless.** This is another way of saying that being a wonderful teacher will make your class better—with no practical suggestions on how to make it happen.

- **It's probably coming from the wrong person.** Many of the teachers who spew this self-serving advice are unrealistic about their own practices. The evidence? They just passed up an opportunity to teach *you* something meaningful, and they made you feel worse in the process.

How to Make It Easier to Do

- **Sorry, this one isn't easy.** Keep teaching and constantly work to make yourself and your classroom better until one day you realize that your classroom culture is supportive—most of the time—and generally encourages respect, responsibility, hard work, and achievement. Then, when people ask you the secret to managing a classroom, say something more helpful than this.

PHASE II
Taking Matters into Your Own Hands

When other teachers talk about the bad kid in their class, you think, "Kid? You mean there's only *one* bad kid?" Consequence King, Consequence Prince, and the growing Consequence Empire are turning your classroom into a carnival. It seems the only reason they come to school is to torment you. You dread having to address their behavior because the whole class turns around to see their reaction. They ignore you. They talk back. They jump to each other's defense, so you are always outnumbered. Parent phone calls have barely made a dent in this group's behavior, and you have already written more referrals than you expected to over the course of the whole year. None of your consequences seem to scare this group and none of your rewards motivate them. Your small bag of tricks has been used up.

Realistic Rewards

To motivate students, you first have to figure out what they want.

Finding the perfect incentive takes time, but it helps to know that most rewards fall into a few tried-and-true categories.

Individual Rewards

Recognition   For some students, this means being able to look at their classmates and say, "Ha ha, losers, I beat you!" For others, it means being a hero—having other students know that the class has gained something because of their efforts. Compliment students or use their work as an example. Make positive phone calls home. Start a list of "winners" and add students to it as they accomplish their goals. Have an "award ceremony" if you are organized enough to make it happen.

Special privileges   For younger students, let them be "line leader" or give them another popular class job. For older ones, print homework passes on dark-colored paper. Let kids sit in a comfortable chair or use the computer. Invite them to eat lunch in the room and bring their friends. Often your best source of reward ideas is listening to the favors kids ask for. Who knew third-graders would work so hard for five minutes of drawing-on-the-board time?

Extra credit   For some reason, students who don't do their regular work will still do anything for extra credit, even though it's usually not worth as much as the assignments they miss. Be careful, though. Extra credit can be a slippery slope toward grade inflation. If you find that students are getting higher grades than they deserve, avoid offering full assignment grades for extra-credit work. Instead, add ten points to the day's assignment, or record extra credit on a separate list and deal with it at the end of the quarter.

Shameless bribes   Yes, I know, learning is its own reward. If, in your first year, you are unable to make students see knowledge for the prize it is, bring candy. Keep a lifetime supply of stickers in your desk. Buy a roll of tickets from the office supply store and give them out to reward kids for staying on task. Then raffle off a small prize each week or a large prize at the end of the quarter. If other teachers tell you they "don't believe in bribing kids," organize a thorough search of their classroom before taking their word for it.

Group Rewards

All of the above   Most incentives that work for individuals can apply to groups with a few adjustments.

More freedom   If one group is making you especially happy, let members choose their seats or work together on an individual assignment. Leaving the room before other students is another effective group prize.

Whole-Class Rewards

Most of the above   With a few exceptions, both individual and group rewards can be adapted for a whole class.

More fun/less work   The chance to earn a large reward, like a pizza party or movie day, can motivate a whole class. Other rewards are simpler, like playing classical music while students work. You can reward older students for a good day with five minutes of that "free time" they keep asking about. The simplest way of doing this is to say, "When I can see you have all learned this, the rest of the period is yours." Then, if students are on task, end the lesson a few minutes early and let them talk.

In-Class Consequences

First know this: getting mad is not a consequence. Yelling can be an effective way to get kids' attention or make them *think* you are upset. However, if students don't care how you feel—and they often don't—yelling actually replaces a real consequence. Consequences, by definition, make students unhappy while you stay relatively calm. The categories below won't replace parent contact and the occasional more serious punishment. However, they are immediate and relatively easy—and you're more likely to be consistent when consequences don't feel like a punishment for you.

Individual Consequences

Private conversation   Confronting a student or demanding answers in front of a class often results in silence or attitude. Find a private time to have the same conversation. You may get the answer or change you want.

Reflective writing   Making students write Bart Simpson–style lines until their hands hurt is, in some states, considered corporal punishment. However, no one says kids can't write essays on discipline-related topics: "Why it is important to be quiet when others are talking," "How homework helps me succeed," "Why I don't need to shake everyone's hand when I walk in late." The possibilities are endless. Critics of this idea say writing should never be used as a punishment, but I disagree. Writing forces kids to reflect, and if students want to explain their tardiness or behavior, they can do it in their essay. If anyone complains, remember: it's not a punishment. It's a "learning tool."

Losing free time   Lunch detentions, after-school detentions, staying a few minutes after the bell—anything that makes students sit silently with their teacher instead of being loud with their friends is an effective consequence. The drawback, of course, is that you have to keep students from skipping their detentions. Then you have to spend your own free time with someone who was irritating you earlier. You decide if the trade-off is worth it.

Some teachers give detentions when students miss homework or fail a quiz, then use the extra hour to review. Focusing on students' progress makes you the good guy during your time with them and often improves in-class behavior.

Isolation   You can curb side conversations by temporarily moving students to a desk next to yours, in a back corner, or facing away from the class. You can also talk to colleagues about holding disruptive kids, but don't overdo this unless you return the favor.

Anything that says "Don't make me..."   Don't underestimate the power of the teacher look. It's not technically a consequence, but it keeps you from having to use up real punishments on minor offenses. Standing next to talking students or tapping their desks while you're teaching also falls into this category. One teacher says she walks around with a notebook as students work and stops every now and then to make "notes." Kids have no idea what she's doing, but they stay on task.

Group or Whole-Class Consequences

Taking away free time   For younger kids, post recess or free time and take minutes off for bad behavior. For secondary students, put thirty seconds on the board every time you have to stop class for an interruption. Then make kids sit in silence after the bell. Avoid conflicts with students and other teachers by keeping the total time under two minutes, especially if students have to get to another class.

Making class less fun   As the teacher, you reserve the right to end fun activities. If students don't act right during a game or discussion, switch to book work. If you can't get through a lesson, stop and give a pop quiz. Build up activity levels slowly as students prove they can handle the change.

Getting completely quiet   Stopping in the middle of a sentence and looking mad is the equivalent of giving the teacher look to the whole class. If students know you have more unpleasant consequences up your sleeve, they will tell each other to be quiet. They may not know exactly what's coming, but they don't want to find out.

PHASE III
Taking Charge of an Out-of-Control Class

The worst part about hitting rock bottom is you don't know you've hit rock bottom. You hate the sound of your alarm clock. You hate the fact that you didn't just die in your sleep, and now you have to go in and face these kids. Consequence King no longer stands out as your worst student—the rest of the class, with a few exceptions, has risen to his challenge.

At this point, the only way you can possibly get your class's attention is to yell louder than they are yelling—no easy task. Even then, there is a good chance they will either yell back or ignore you completely. By the time the bell rings, half your students are outside and the other half are pushing to get through the door. You spend an hour after they leave making your room presentable enough for the custodian. One day, while cleaning, you discover someone has peed in the trash can.

The worst part about this—as if you could pick a worst part—is that a few of the students are genuinely nice kids. They ignore paper balls flying past their heads, open their books when you tell them to, and do things that look like wanting to learn. You hear other students calling them names. One day a paper ball hits your nicest student in the back of the head. He doesn't even turn around. It hurts you that you cannot protect him.

Things are constantly being thrown across the room—paper, loud insults, casual threats, and a constant stream of curse words, sometimes directed at you. Textbooks are ripped up and covered with writing. Lights get turned off. You regularly find things missing from your desk. Sometimes you wonder if the class would act better with no adult in the room at all.

If this sounds like your situation, hearing about the importance of classroom management makes you lose your appetite. You have already realized you need most of the class on your side for a standard management system to work. You already know what you should have done better, or earlier, or whatever. You just need something to help you fix this. Now.

A class that is completely out of control is most teachers' worst nightmare, but it does offer you a certain freedom. At this point, you have nowhere to go but up. Give yourself permission to stray from the curriculum and teach almost anything that will get students' attention. Work to make your class see itself as a team. They need to see that you care and they need a reason to change, so focus your energy on finding that reason. Look at it this way: what are they learning now?

While there is no guaranteed cure for an off-the-wall class, enough teachers have bounced back from insanity to share some ideas:

" *One Monday I put 500 points on the board and told my students this was their 'participation grade' for the week. Every time a cell phone rang, someone forgot their book, or kids started talking, I took ten points off. When I saw something I liked, I added ten points. At the end of the week, if there were 450 points on the board, they got an A for participation. I told them, 'Eventually, I will treat you as individuals, but right now all I can see is a whole class not doing what it should be.' I knew it was working when they started telling each other to shut up.* **"**

❝*My seventh period was my worst class and they knew it. I forced myself to pretend I liked them. I would say things like 'I'm really happy. You know why? Because it's seventh period!' They looked at me like I was crazy, but I could tell they liked hearing it. Eventually they calmed down.***❞**

❝*My sixth-graders' behavior had been slipping for a while, but we went to the park for a school event. On the way back, we passed a sprinkler and every single student got out of line and ran into the water. I yelled at them to come back, but they just ignored me until they saw me walking toward the school without them. I had to pass my principal with a line of loud, soaking-wet kids. The next day, I kept the class completely quiet the whole day. They did nothing but book work. It took a few weeks before we did any fun activities, but when we did, they were much better.***❞**

❝*Around January, my class calmed down. I don't know exactly why. It's like they just said to themselves, 'We're not going to be evil anymore,' and they weren't.***❞**

A Few Things to Consider Before Planning a Hostile Takeover

- Timing is important. The best time for a major change is when you haven't seen your students for a few days. If you can't wait until break, at least start on a Monday.

- Sometimes you need one especially problematic student out of the room in order to fix things. If this is the case, plan how and when to make it happen. Ask another teacher to hold the student for a few days, or write a referral and follow up until he/she is suspended. Then, plan how to hold onto progress when this student comes back.

- Going crazy can help...or backfire. Some teachers suggest going absolutely nuts—or at least doing something so out of character that kids think they've pushed you past your breaking point. If this works, it's because the shock value gives you a chance to reinvent your personality. Remember, though, you only get one freak-out per year, in one class. Word travels fast with students, and they will never take you seriously a second time.

- Getting your kids to "JUST SHUT UP!!!!!!" is only the first step. You will still need a solid system to keep from sliding back to square zero. Any new system you try will be tested repeatedly before kids believe you are serious. Be prepared to hold on tight as kids try to shake off the new routine.

- If you don't give up, time is on your side. Classes that have run off past teachers are surprised when you continue to walk in every morning and try to teach. Change may not happen as fast as you want it to, but students often calm down over time just because you're still around.

- Your students want to be in a well-run classroom. Even when their actions suggest otherwise, your students want you to regain control. Some of your behavior problems are actually following the lead of other students. Once you establish yourself as a leader, you can convince them to follow you.

8

POPULAR PROCEDURES THAT (PROBABLY) PREVENT PROBLEMS

*U*ndoubtedly you've heard the classic teacher advice "Beg, borrow, and steal." A better phrase would be, "Beg, borrow, steal…and then adapt." This is especially true with classroom procedures. Other teachers can share the basic principles behind their routines, but rarely can they pass on details developed over years of trial and error. If another teacher's routines fall flat the first time you try them, don't get discouraged. These procedures are inseparable from a teacher's personality and are almost always more complex than they sound.

Consider this chapter a starter kit of procedures to borrow, steal, and then adapt. Each section contains tips from experienced teachers.

STARTING CLASS

The sooner you start class after the bell, the better students understand that the bell means class has started. Say good morning immediately and make moves to show that class is in session. Give directions. Enforce rules. Try not to let distractions slow you down. Your procedures should include a reason for students to be seated and silent as quickly as possible. This doesn't mean they'll be as on task as you want them to be. It just means you won't have to wait for an opening while kids walk in late and loud.

Meeting Students at the Door

66*Attendance does not have to be the first thing you do each class. Whenever possible, kill two birds with one stone. Utilize the time while students are filing into class to collect homework or pass back graded papers. If you have handouts to distribute, pass them out as you greet your students at the door. Try to deal with individual problems after the dismissal bell. The time when students are engaged in seatwork is another good time to take attendance or deal with individual students. Housekeeping chores can always wait. Grabbing students' attention cannot.*99

Starting Class with Silence (Somewhat)

66*From the beginning of the year, I make it clear that students have a job to do as soon as they walk in. There is always a journal topic on the board, and kids know they have fifteen minutes to get their journals from the cabinet and write at least twenty lines. I don't check the work every day, but I collect journals every ten classes and they only get credit for complete entries. As they finish writing, I put the next set of directions on the overhead projector. This procedure takes some monitoring at first, but once students understand it, I use those beautiful minutes of silence to check homework, take attendance, or collect my thoughts before moving on to more active segments of the lesson.*99

Dealing with Unprepared Students

66*I have gone through various methods of dealing with unprepared students. When I first began teaching, I set up a system in which students could borrow* *pencils from me if they left collateral. The good news was I always got my pencils back. The problem was that unprepared students would line up at my desk, and sometimes they would want to exchange something like a shoe as collateral, which caused a big unnecessary distraction at the beginning of class. I then tried a system in which students could simply borrow paper and pencils from a big box at the front of the room. This took less time, but kids began treating my room like an office supply store. I abandoned the system when I gave an assignment to my eighth period and more than half of the students rushed up to the front of the room to borrow paper. Now, I make no mention of providing any supplies to students and have noticed that they generally just borrow supplies from one another if they need to. Occasionally a student will ask to borrow a pencil from me, and I will fish one out of my desk drawer and say something like, 'This is my favorite pencil, so you better do really fantastic work today.' This has been my favorite system so far, even though it's not much of a system at all.* **"**

STUDENT PARTICIPATION

Student participation is a balancing act. You want kids to get excited, but you don't want them to interrupt. You want good answers, but you don't want the same student answering every question. You want to keep kids on their toes, but not to put them on the spot. Much of your method for calling on students depends on how much structure you can impose…or how much excitement you can handle.

Using Cards to Call on Students

"*At the beginning of the year I tape playing cards to each desk to divide students into teams. I keep a corresponding deck of cards in my desk. Whenever I ask a question, students get a moment to discuss it with their group. Then I pick a card to decide who answers. If the answer is correct, the whole group gets* a point or reward. If the chosen kid says, 'Huh? What was the question?' his whole group stands up until they have another chance to prove themselves. This puts pressure on everyone to pay attention, and kids who know the answer get a chance to share it with their teammates. After students answer, their cards go back in the deck so they know they can be called on again. **"**

Keeping Up the Energy

"Early in my career, I realized I didn't care much whether students raised their hands. I would rather keep the energy going, even if it means letting students call out answers. Sometimes I ask a question and tell the class, 'I want five different examples from five different students.' Then I hold up my hand and count off each good answer I hear, repeating the answer at the same time to reinforce it. This doesn't work perfectly, of course. Sometimes I have to limit the number of times enthusiastic students are allowed to call out answers. Other times, the class gets too loud and I tell them their answers are good, but I'm getting a headache. Then I make them raise their hands for the rest of the day. **"**

Cheating the System, a Little

"I had a few kids who waved their hands in the air after every question. The rest of the class just spaced out. One coworker told me she called on kids randomly by writing their names on Popsicle sticks and pulling them from a cup. This solved my original problem, but sometimes I asked a hard question and then picked the names of five struggling students in a row. When no one knew the answer, it slowed down my lessons and embarrassed my low kids. I asked my coworker about this. She laughed and said, 'Usually you want to be fair, but when you really need to move on, that Popsicle stick says whatever name you need it to.' **"**

GROUP WORK

Ahhh, group work. Students love it for the same reason we don't:

it generally involves a whole lot of group and not much work. This is not to say you should never do it. Just keep a few things in mind.

Waiting Until Kids Can Handle It

"*I start group work late in the year, after students have proven they can stay on task alone. I walk around with my class list on a clipboard and tell kids I'm taking off points if they get loud or off topic. I also tell them they're getting both a group and individual grade. Most of the time, I'm lying. The truth is we only do group work when I think kids will learn more even if they do get off task—because they will.***"**

Grading Group Behavior

"*When groups give presentations, I include an 'audience score' in their grades. If they talk through another group's speech, their team loses points.***"**

Discouraging Freeloaders

"*My biggest problem with group work was that one student often did the work while the rest of the group got the same grade for doing nothing. There are a few ways I now try to prevent this. Sometimes I break up assignments so everyone has a different job. The worksheet for each job is different so kids can't copy. For short group assignments, I say everyone's handwriting must be on the paper, and students must put their names next to their contributions.***"**

EDUCATIONAL GAMES AND TEAM-BUILDING ACTIVITIES

Your plan for the day includes an educational review game. The kids get excited. Then they get loud. Then a question about who had their hand up first or who was whispering the answer makes everyone forget the purpose of the activity. Your class turns into a who-can-yell-the-loudest contest. You lose.

Does this sound familiar? Maybe it happened the first time you let kids play a game. Maybe it's in the back of your mind keeping you from even trying. Games are a great way of reinforcing what students learn, but they are also a classroom management risk. You need to decide if your class can handle it.

Introducing Games Gradually

"*I learned the hard way not to let my classes play games until I'm happy with their everyday behavior. Then I introduce contests and games a little at a time. If kids get out of hand, I shut the game down and we do something boring. (In fact, I usually do this on purpose the first time we play.) I also try to schedule games near the end of class. Once kids are hyperactive and worked up, it's much easier to send them somewhere else than calm them down for a lesson.***"*

Revising and Reviewing the Rules

"*Rules evolve a little each time we play a game, but we always review before we start. The one rule that never changes is that I am the referee, and the referee is always right.***"*

THE BATHROOM LINE

For grade school teachers, the bathroom line is like a classroom management parade. As fifty students wait to use four tiny toilets, teachers with well-behaved lines enjoy the luxury of talking to adults. Their "line monitors" mark clipboards every time a child uncrosses an arm, turns a head, or even thinks about whispering.

On the other end of the spectrum are the line-competition losers. These teachers run back and forth themselves, shrieking at kids to stop-leaning-on-the-wall-stop-talking-keep-your-hands-to-yourself-turn-around-I-said-stop-talking-etc. As they pass each section of the line, students directly behind them go back to what they were doing.

Heaven help you if another teacher has to stop his or her conversation to put your class in check. Another teacher correcting your class in front of you is like someone offering to make dinner for your spouse on your anniversary. It is an indirect way of saying, "You're not handling your own business, so I guess I have to." If it's unnecessary, it can make you stay mad for the whole day. If it is necessary, it's even worse.

Making a Big Deal out of Details

❝ *The first day of school, we practice lining up inside the room. We don't walk out the door until the line is perfect. Faces must be forward. Mouths must be shut. Arms are folded to prevent pushing. When we're walking, students follow a line on the floor and keep one foot on each side of this line at all times. I tell them in advance I won't correct them in the hallway unless absolutely necessary, but all consequences will be doubled when we get back to class. It sounds harsh on paper, but with thirty-three kids in one class, the bathroom line is no time to hold back those anal-retentive tendencies.* **❞**

Dealing with Emergencies

❝ *A kid peed in his pants my first year because I wouldn't let him go to the restroom. After that, I felt so guilty I gave him unlimited bathroom privileges. That backfired, too, because all day, I had kids coming up to me saying, 'It's an emergency.' They all perfected the meaningful I-have-to-go look and emergency leg cross. The next year, I went back to saying no to individual bathroom requests and everyone was fine. It's still a judgment call, though. Every now and then, I make an exception for students with that emergency look in their eyes.* **❞**

Getting By on Your Own Supplies

66 *Our school restrooms are notorious for missing basic supplies, so I keep two baskets next to the door with toilet paper and hand sanitizer. One girl and one boy are in charge of bringing these along on bathroom breaks. I've even started putting hand sanitizer on my supply list at the beginning of the school year, although I'm still too shy to ask for toilet paper.* 99

Timing Bathroom Breaks

66 *My students were taking a long time in the bathroom, and other classes were complaining. I suspected much of that extra time was spent throwing wet toilet paper at the ceiling, so I started timing their breaks. I told students that they had a certain amount of free time each week—they could spend it either moving slowly in the restroom or playing at recess. They got ten minutes per bathroom break, and when we got back to class, we added leftover time to the 'recess board.' Marks for bad conduct took one minute off the total. Every Friday, we added up the recess time and went to play. If the class had negative time at the end of the week, they had to sit silently at their desks, arms folded and heads straight, until they made up the time they owed. This system cut my students' break time in half. Yes, timing students in the bathroom takes a toll on their dignity, but so does a teacher leaning her head into the boys' restroom to scream, 'HURRY UP IN THERE, JAVIER!!!!'* 99

Keeping Student Behavior in Line

66 *The idea of having a line monitor has always seemed like an ethical dilemma to me. I want a well-behaved line, but I don't want my helpers to become targets of resentment. Right now I have a monitor who saves kids from consequences instead of writing down names. I hold the clipboard myself and write down names of those who misbehave. If the line monitor corrects the behavior and it*

stops immediately, there is no consequence. This has worked well so far, and it makes me the bad guy instead of putting a kid in that position. **99**

HALL PASSES FOR OLDER STUDENTS

After switching from elementary to high school, I beamed at the thought of never having to walk students to the bathroom again. My smile disappeared when I realized thirty students would now interrupt my lesson every time they had to go.

Limiting Passes

66 *Each of my students gets two bathroom passes per nine-week marking period. Passes are a new color each marking period, and unused passes from previous marking periods can be used for either bathroom or homework passes. At the end of the year, students can turn in all of their unused passes for extra credit. In most cases, the increasing value is enough encouragement for students to save their passes when possible. In the few cases where students have used up their passes and claim to have an emergency, I tell them they can go, but will lose one letter grade from the day's assignment. This prevents a forced confrontation; students who have a genuine emergency happily accept the offer. Most wait for the bell.* **99**

Making Passes Inconvenient

66 *The bigger and heavier you make your hall pass, the less fun it is for students to wander the halls with it. The prize for this one goes to a woodshop teacher at my school. His students walk through the hall wearing a 4' × 4' sandwich board!* **99**

ENFORCING CONSEQUENCES

Sometimes teachers think their consequences are ineffective when the real problem is their system for enforcing those consequences.

We've all heard the story of the mother who punishes her child and says, "It hurts me more than it hurts you." This should not be the case in your classroom. Students should believe consequences hurt them significantly more than they hurt you. The ultimate goal is to establish a rhythm that lets you enforce rules without stopping class at all.

Letting Students Save Face

❝ *If another teacher asks me what I do about cell phones, I say, 'If I see or hear a phone, I take it until the end of the school day.' Technically, I won't take it myself unless it's on a student's desk. In other cases, I calmly tell the student to turn the phone off and give it to me. Then I turn my attention elsewhere for about a minute before turning back and holding out my hand. If I spot someone text-messaging or hear a phone from across the room, I say, 'Please turn off your phone before you put it on my desk.' Saying this in a firm but calm voice works 99 percent of the time, and if it doesn't, I send the student to in-school suspension. If I don't know whose phone is ringing and no one comes forward, I write '30 seconds' on the board, and the kids know they will have to stay after class. Then I drop the subject. I know this system isn't foolproof, because at the end of every year, kids tell me, 'Ha-ha, I sent text messages in your class a bunch of times and you never saw me!' They feel slick because they never got caught. I feel slick because what they don't know is I don't care if they got away with sending a text message. I care that cell phones never became a disruption in my class.* **❞**

Becoming a Broken Record

❝ *I used to add extra consequences if a child argued with me, but this often escalated the situation. Now I just repeat my original instructions, broken-record style, until the student complies. (Okay, you need a late pass from the office.*

Mmmhmmm. You need a late pass from the office. Okay. You need…) Arguing with students means we are justifying our actions to them in front of the class. We don't owe troublemakers a public hearing. **99**

Giving Mini-Consequences

66*Not all misbehavior needs to be addressed with a full consequence. For example, some of my students try to save a trip to the garbage by crumpling their paper into basketballs. I've never actually set a rule to prevent this, but if a student aims at the trash and misses, I say, 'Make sure you pick up all the other papers near the garbage while you're picking up yours.' Cleaning the area around the trash can is enough community service, in my opinion, to make up for a minor offense. Plus, the whole class knows the student missed the shot. Justice served.* **99**

Knowing What You Can Get Away With

66*When students fall asleep in my class, I spray them with water. I've had other teachers at my school say they would never do this because it could cause a confrontation, but I've never had a major problem. I never spray students in the face or on the hair, and don't let students spray each other. This is not something I'd recommend to every teacher. It's just something that has worked well in my classes. Students even point out sleeping classmates just to watch them get sprayed!* **99**

THE LAST FIVE MINUTES

It's important to tell students early in the year: "The bell does not dismiss this class. I do." Otherwise you'll end lessons to the sweet sound of students slamming books and shoving each other into the hallway. Then you will get to clean up the mess they left behind— not the most rewarding way to end your day.

Incorporating Cleanup Time

"*I check that desks are straight and papers are off the floor before dismissing the class. I do this as the bell rings, so students know it's their responsibility to straighten up ahead of time. If the room is not clean, all students stay until it is. Some students will sit and watch others do their dirty work, so I occasionally let students leave early for cleaning up garbage that's not theirs. At the same time, I try to show respect for the kids' time by wrapping up early enough to let them gather their things. If it's my fault a lesson ran over, I let the class pack up before I finish, then talk until the bell and dismiss them on time.***"**

Rewarding Readiness

"*When my students get ready to leave at the end of the day, I let the cleanest, quietest sections line up first. I used to try to keep kids quiet while they packed, but then decided I didn't care. It's the end of the day anyway.***"**

9

THE DUE-DATE BLUES: WHEN HIGH EXPECTATIONS MEET LOW MOTIVATION

*N*othing looks better on paper than the advice "Set high expectations for your students." Politicians, in-service presenters, and countless books with apples on their covers insist that students will rise to meet the standards we set. Most beginning teachers already know high expectations are important. Few are prepared for the low skill levels standing in the way or for the advanced strategies kids use to avoid hard work.

Picture this: you spend days designing a research project that is both demanding and creative, teaching essential skills while also appealing to a variety of learning styles. You discuss it every day for weeks and give students plenty of class time to work on it. You even stay during lunch and after school in case anyone comes by for help.

On the due date, you feel like someone has punched you in the stomach. Only six kids turn in projects. Of the six, three are in 29-point type, filled with obvious spelling mistakes, and only loosely connected to the directions. One is half-typed and half-handwritten because the student "tried to finish during lunch" but "had to eat." One-third of your class is absent, and five students are at your desk telling you their printers ran out of ink. Three hand you notes from their "parents." The rest give you their best impression of being so, so sorry because they "totally forgot," but you notice everyone starting to get that look in their eyes that says, "Hey! No one did it! We're not the only losers in here!" You fight the urge to grab the class in a group choke hold and clap their heads together like cymbals. Welcome to the due-date blues.

SYMPTOMS OF THE DUE-DATE BLUES

Signs you may be infected with due-date blues include violent feelings, a general sense of hopelessness, and nagging questions such as the following:

- After I design an assignment that pushes kids' limits, how do I get them to do it?

- Do I have to grade on a curve to reward the few kids who made the effort? What if their work sucks?

- Do I refuse late work to teach responsibility, or accept it so I have something to put in my grade book?

- How do I motivate kids to achieve great things when so many of them are satisfied with just passing?

- How do I punish the kids who don't even come to class on the due date?

- I want to motivate my kids using positive reinforcement and goal setting, but it doesn't seem to be working. Is it okay to scare kids into learning? (By the way, how *do* I scare kids into learning?)

TREATING THE DUE-DATE BLUES

Some teachers will tell you to forget about assigning homework or big projects because students won't do them anyway. Comments like these reflect years of frustration, and there is often some truth to them. At the same time, most successful people have had to sweat to meet deadlines—chances are your own school career included an all-nighter or two. You owe it to students to assign projects that push their limits. You owe them clear directions and help if necessary. Then you owe it to yourself to make students feel just as miserable as you do if they don't bother to try.

If a few students did the assignment, avoid going crazy on the whole class. Kids feel relieved, not ashamed, when they are part of a large group in trouble together. Instead, praise the work you received. Find a group reward for those who did it. Then find a consequence that makes each student feel alone in the decision to fail. Here are a few of your treatment options:

- **Bring treats on the due date**. Let those who did the assignment eat candy or snacks in front of those who didn't.

- **Think about whether quality is a battle you want to fight right now**. If it is, hand back unacceptable work and give students one more day to improve it. If not, don't mention quality until grading time.

- **Consider what percentage of students did the work.** If more than half did it, give the unprepared students a long, silent assignment while other kids talk—I mean "peer edit." If only a few students did the work, write them a pass to the library or send them to another room while you conduct essay-writing boot camp for everyone else. The justification for this is that these students already learned what they were supposed to. Now they can afford some free time.

- **Plan presentations productively.** If kids are doing presentations, consider taking volunteers first. You can even offer to grade the first few presenters more generously. Keep unprepared or unenthusiastic students from hurting the momentum of the rest of the class by leaving them—and your corresponding consequences—for last.

Conscientious kids can lose steam if they know they're performing for classmates who didn't do the work.

- **Review your policy for late work.** If you told kids you don't take late work, you have every right to stand by your word. In some cases, though, you may feel the chance of pulling in a few extra assignments is worth a (totally inconsistent) change in policy. If you do decide to backtrack, show consideration for kids who met the deadline by giving them extra credit or knocking grades off late work.

- **Make parent contact manageable.** You may want to call the homes of all students who missed an assignment. When this involves just a few phone calls, it's a good idea. In other cases, this means staying at school long after dark to call thirty sets of parents, nineteen of whom will say something like, "Oh, is there anything she can do to make it up? No? Oh, well, um...I'll talk to her." In these cases, it may be better to whittle down your parent contact list strategically. It is okay to call only the parents of students you repeatedly reminded about the assignment, students whose grades dropped as a result of missing the work, or students who didn't show up on the due date. If you decide to extend a deadline and offer students a chance to do the work for a late grade, you may want to call only when students do not take advantage of the second opportunity.

- **Make students write their own failure notices.** Dictating failure notices and having students write them down makes a productive outlet for due-date blues anger. After all, you're just giving the lecture you would have given anyway. Writing means students have to actually listen. Even better, they're looking at their desks instead of staring at you or smirking at their friends while you talk. You can also skip the lecture by typing the notice ahead of time. Keep a folder full in your classroom for students to copy as needed. A typical notice might sound like this:

  "Today was the due date of a major project. I had more than

a month to complete this project. It was worth _____ grade(s). This assignment was a way to prepare me to be a successful adult with the skills needed to hold a job I will enjoy. I knew from the day it was assigned that it would be difficult, if not impossible, for me to pass this class without completing this project. My teacher was available to help me during lunch every day this week in case I had any problems. Computers are available in the school library, which closes at 8:00 p.m. I understand that being successful in life involves meeting deadlines and doing things I don't always feel like doing. My success or failure in life is my responsibility. I chose failure over hard work on this project."

Make sure to include all details relevant to the assignment, and give students a chance to add their own comments before signing and dating the letters. Then file the papers in students' record files in case you need them during a parent conference. You can also offer students the opportunity to make up the assignment for a late grade once they have finished copying the notice.

- **Make them do it anyway.** Sometimes circumstances leave you with no choice but to let unprepared students make up work during class time. In these cases, have them work in an isolated spot while other students peer edit or do a fun or extra credit activity. The advantage of this is that it gives students some hope of catching up long term. It also keeps them on the hook for completing their work and lets you offer help if you see that it is needed. Work done in class, however, should generally be marked two grades off: one for being late, and one for the opportunity to work in class.

PREVENTING FUTURE OUTBREAKS OF DUE-DATE BLUES

When the due-date blues hit, your first instinct is to blame yourself. Was the assignment understandable? Were directions clear?

Did you give enough reminders? It's important to consider these questions, but the due date of a major project is no time to show self-doubt. Students must learn it's their responsibility to get work done by a deadline and get help if they need it. The reality is that some students chose to skip the project on the day you assigned it, and showing insecurity sends the message they made the right choice. That said, there *are* some changes that might improve your numbers next time:

- **Make it competitive.** Post turn-in percentages for each class or group. Bring a treat for the winners and leave numbers up until the next major due date.

- **Be as clear as possible.** Provide typed, numbered directions for all projects. Then review in class to make sure every step is clear. Asking, "Any questions?" isn't enough. Make kids explain instructions in their own words.

- **Be available to help.** Let students know where and when they can find you if they're stuck. Give homework related to the larger project. This will help students keep up and give them a chance to fix misunderstandings before the last minute.

- **Hold kids accountable.** Make students sign contracts so they know what the assignment is, when it is due, and how to get help if they need it.

- **Count down to the due date.** Write project due dates on the board and leave them up. Mention them every day. Post a daily countdown. Show students how to use their assignment planners or cell phone calendars to plan backward from a final due date and set smaller deadlines along the way.

- **Monitor progress.** Have kids fill out sheets once a week stating what they've accomplished so far and what they plan to do over the weekend. This also teaches them planning skills and reminds them large projects are not meant to be done overnight.

- **Break it into pieces.** Have a rough-draft due date, an outline due date, a due date for notes, et cetera. The more separate deadlines involved, the higher your numbers will be for the final draft. If you plan to contact parents when kids don't turn in a project, call on the earlier due dates. That way, when they ask, "Is there anything he can do about it?" the answer will still be yes.

DESIGNING FOOLPROOF(ER) ASSIGNMENTS

After dealing with the quantity of work you didn't get, it's time to face the quality of work you got. Prepare for more pain. Students are great at doing the easy or creative parts of assignments, then skipping requirements that test real knowledge. I'd live pretty comfortably if I had a dollar for every horribly written essay printed on decorative paper. If I got paid for obvious plagiarism, I could certainly afford to quit teaching. It's hard to plug every loophole students use to escape from learning. However, teachers can take various steps to make directions clearer and force students to work at the top of their ability:

- **Distribute rubrics or checklists for all major assignments.** Rubrics should describe what skills you're grading for and how many points each category is worth. You may want to include categories for neatness, completion, and effort.
- **Review directions early and often.** Give a quiz or play a game based on directions. Draw connections between daily activities and long-term projects. On your rough-draft due date, students should spot-check each other's work using the checklist you've provided.
- **Make students predict their own grades.** Include a blank column on your rubric for students to estimate their own grades before turning in their projects. *Is the paper typed in 12-point font? Did you get the five points for correctly labeling all literary devices?* Students should be able to answer these questions themselves before turning in work

for a grade—and adjust the quality of their work to get the grade they want.

- **Discuss plagiarism.** Make sure students recognize cheating in all its forms. Then discuss how seriously you and other teachers take it. Plagiarism causes students to flunk college classes and destroys the careers of adults. All universities and even some high schools subscribe to services like Turnitin.com, which checks student work against every piece of printed material on the Internet. Ask if your school subscribes, but also give assignments that are difficult to copy and paste from a website. The days of two-page biographies are over.

WHY THE DUE-DATE BLUES MAKE TEACHERS SO SICK

When students skip assignments, it shows more than a casual attitude toward failure. It shows they missed the whole point of what we're doing here. Teachers don't really need eye-catching poster boards explaining the scientific method. If we did, we could easily have made them ourselves. We demand quality work because we want kids to know how to create quality. We teach kids good behavior hoping they will become good people. Our real goal is for students to absorb values that will turn them into happy, honest, successful people, one eye-catching poster board at a time.

Ten Principles of Successful Living We All Hope Students Learn from Us

1. Be where you're supposed to be, on time and prepared.
2. Follow all steps of directions.
3. Think for yourself, and do the right thing even when no one's watching.
4. Think about the future and how your present actions affect it.
5. Take responsibility for your decisions.

6. Search for solutions instead of complaining about problems.

7. Show respect and expect respect back.

8. Present yourself as an intelligent person.

9. Produce a finished product that won't need any explaining.

10. Put more into the world than you take out.

10

NO CHILD LEFT... YEAH, YEAH, YOU KNOW: DIFFERENT TYPES OF STUDENTS AND WHAT EACH TYPE NEEDS FROM YOU

*I*n teacher movies, the real problem is always motivation. Behavior issues fade as the teacher finds a way to get through to students, and they take off like grateful, street-smart rockets. Real-life teachers find that, while motivation is an issue for many kids, others try hard without success. Students who understand effortlessly may be rude to struggling classmates, while others disrupt because they are struggling themselves. Some kids have no discipline at home. Some have too much. Some are switching schools next week. The resulting combination is much harder to push toward a happy ending.

If the movies are right about one thing though, it's this: the heart of teaching is forming relationships with students as we move them from point A to point B. Sometimes, the bonds form as we push children toward their goals. Other times, we have to earn some credibility before they trust us to lead the way.

Teachers care about kids. It's what we do. At the same time, students are people, and we don't get along equally with all people. Deep down, many of us had a specific type of child in mind when we chose this career. Maybe we're drawn to kids who remind us of younger versions of ourselves. Other times, it's the thug with the neck tattoo who shows his soft side during our poetry unit, the struggling sweetheart whose eyes light up when she gets the answer, the smart kid who's never felt challenged. Then there's the honor-roll superstar who finishes her work early and loves to help us with ours. We may not always trust her intentions, but we sure do appreciate her positive attitude and all that help.

On the other hand, we sometimes have kids we don't like: bullies, eye-rollers, girls who look like younger versions of our ex's new girlfriend, et cetera. We know we shouldn't have favorites, but certain kids make our day, while others just make our day harder. Part of our job is figuring out how to build relationships with the kids in our classrooms, even those who frustrate us. In the end, they all need to get from point A to point B, and we're in charge of the transportation.

LOW-PERFORMING KIDS
Why They Break Your Heart

You will quickly realize point A is not the same for every child. Working with some students feels like trying to build a sand castle where the waves hit the shore. Your explanations and extra help are never enough. Progress seems to wash away without a trace. The saddest part is that these students follow all the rules you've invented to guard against careless mistakes. These students are not careless, though. They do all the test-taking strategies, copy all the notes. They make mistakes because they just don't get it. How do you make life fair for students who do everything you ask of them and still don't come out on top?

66 *There was a girl in my math class who would raise her hand after every explanation and say, 'I...don't...get it.' Every day, several times a day, I would see that hand in the air and this pained look on her face. My stomach muscles would tighten because I knew what she was going to say. She was such a nice girl, but I dreaded calling on her because I couldn't figure out how to make her understand.* **99**

What They Need from You

Patience   Successful or not, we all have at least one thing we do terribly. Personally, I'd be lost if I had to fix my own car, and I can't sing—not even "Happy Birthday." These, of course, are only the weaknesses I'm willing to share in print. Luckily for me, I can avoid doing these things in public or under pressure, and admitting our shortcomings is easy when they don't impact our lives. Struggling students, on the other hand, constantly hear that school success is the key to their future. To put ourselves in their shoes, we need to picture our own weaknesses under the same microscope.

Acronyms, mnemonic devices, and concrete tricks that work every time   Higher-order thinking skills have their time and place, but students need to understand concepts at a basic level before they can build models of them, write poems about them, or use them in word problems. Listen to parents helping kids with homework and you'll still hear some of the mnemonic devices they learned in school for remembering planets, order of operations, colors of the rainbow, and so on. These things work. Borrow them from other teachers or challenge your own students to create memory-friendly phrases.

Recognition when they get it right   Passing a spelling test for the first time doesn't make someone an A student, but your struggling speller doesn't need a reminder of that. Jump up and down. Take a picture. Give him a thousand stickers. He passed his first spelling test! Low-performing kids work hard for those small victories. They need to know that you know it's a big deal.

The "growth mindset"   In her book *Mindset*, psychology professor Carol Dweck shows that people are more successful when they believe ability grows with effort. Instead of complimenting kids by saying they are smart, praise them by saying they worked hard and their efforts paid off. This attitude helps all students, not just low achievers. Students try harder when they know their current report card is not their destiny.

Why Giving Them Your Attention Is Worth It

❝ *One day while we were working on subtraction, I noticed my student kept counting problems on her fingers and ending up one number off. I showed her a trick I learned when I was in school: write the smaller number on a piece of paper, then draw dots as you count up to the higher number. The number of dots is always the correct answer because writing the original number keeps students from counting the starting point. The next day the girl came in early and told me, 'Guess what, Miss? I get subtraction!' I gave her a few problems and she got them all right. It was a huge boost to her confidence...and mine.* **❞**

UNMOTIVATED KIDS
Why They Will Frustrate You

If you need any more proof that life is unfair, move your focus to that bored-looking kid rolling his eyes in the corner. He does nothing unless you come over and place the pencil between his fingers, yet he can knock out a decent paper the night before it's due.

Unlike your struggling students, this kid would love for you to think he's hopelessly stupid. Then you would let him get away with staring at the wall all day and occasionally turning in sloppy twelve-line essays. This kid may not be a genius, but he could clearly be doing better with the tiniest effort. The problem is you can't get him to put in the tiniest effort.

You better figure it out soon, because if you have to say the word *potential* one more time…

"*I had this student my first year who drove me crazy. This student did not care about getting work done or being in school, and he was rude about it. He would come in late every day, sit at his desk, and do nothing, but every now and then he'd call out the correct answer to a question without raising his hand. He did this just enough to let me know he could do the work if he felt like it, which made his lack of effort seem even more like a slap in the face. My second year I got this student again because he did not pass to the next grade. I about died when I saw his name on my roster.***"*

What They Need from You

Impatience   If you know they can do it, and they know they can do it, and they know you know they can do it, stop telling them you know they can do it and make them do it. Then, if it's not done right, make them redo it. Get upset. Raise your voice. Call home with your concerns. Some kids only get lazier when they have a blank check of encouragement. Let them know that they're not as impressive as they think they are and that they still have plenty to prove.

Relevance   I won't insult you by saying, "Well, maybe you should plan lessons around students' interests to get them more involved!" Chances are, you've been trying to do that since day one, and this kid is still drawing pictures on his quizzes.

However, if a student is clearly capable of more than he is achieving, it can't hurt to ask a few questions. Offer an alternate assignment or talk with him privately about how to catch his attention. If all you get is an irritated shrug, at least you know *you* made some effort.

Competition   Kids who won't work for their own benefit may do it to help their classes win a contest or beat another group in a game. In the end, it doesn't matter why they do it as long as they do it.

A reality check   If a student refuses to work despite your best efforts, let him fail. Life doesn't give grades based on potential. Neither should you.

Why Giving Them Your Attention Is Still Worth It

❝ *There have been so many difficult students it's hard to know where to begin, but I'll start with a student I had fifteen years ago in my second year of teaching. He rarely did his work in class, but he wasn't stupid—just indifferent to education. What he did care about was socializing…all day, every day. He drove me crazy with his nonstop talking. After a particularly bad day, I wrote a referral and followed up with his counselor. It turned out he already had 167 referrals in the system! It seemed he was immune to them. I stopped writing him up, but I did stay on his case throughout the school year. Eventually, he dropped out. I didn't think much more about him until he came back to visit a few years later. He told me he had gotten his GED. Then he went to a trade school, got a good job, and was making a nice life for himself. He said he was sorry he had been a disruption in my class. He also wanted me to know he appreciated my efforts to teach him. He knew I tried hard, even if I was somewhat unsuccessful. The lesson I learned from this was that students continue to grow up after they leave us. Sometimes we get them when they are just too young and immature to perform well in the classroom.* **❞**

SHY KIDS
Why You Will Worry About Them

According to questionable statistics on several websites, public speaking is the number-one fear of Americans. Death is number two. If this is true, it means some of our students would rather die than speak up in front of their classmates. They'd certainly rather get the wrong answer on their homework.

"My class emphasized participation and performances. I was proud that the loud kids got involved in the activities instead of disrupting the class. It wasn't until the end of the year I realized some of my quieter students had low grades. One young man in particular never said a word the whole year and didn't turn in any work—I kept getting mad at him and calling him out in public because I thought he was lazy, but his other teachers told me he was a decent student. I never figured out how to get him to do anything and he ended up failing the class. Maybe there was nothing I could have done for this student, but I wish I had provided him and my other shy kids an opportunity to shine."

What They Need from You

The spotlight off them   It is possible to get trapped in silence. If you've ever been the quiet one in a group, you know as soon as someone says, "Hey! How come you're not saying anything?" you are locked out of the conversation for good. There's not a chance you will open your mouth with the added pressure of making up for your silence. Keep this in mind, and think twice before you innocently point the class's attention toward a kid who "hasn't had a chance to participate yet."

Other lines of communication   Teachers, by definition, have overcome our shyness at least enough to speak in front of students. That's not to say we can't relate to our shy kids. It just means we need to be extra careful when interpreting their silence. It's a mistake to assume quiet students have nothing to say, but equally wrong to assume they understand everything. One solution is to pass out index cards and make all students write a question or comment. You can also assign a one-page "letter to the teacher" or ask kids to put stars on journal entries they'd like you to read. Quiet students can take advantage of these opportunities if they want you to know them better.

A reason to come out of their shells   Part of our job is to get students past their limitations. At some point during the year, you should expect even your shyest students to say *something*. The first time is always the hardest, so consider bending the rules: let them present with a friend, read from note cards, or perform sitting down. When they finally speak up, make sure you congratulate them...privately.

Why Giving Them Your Attention Is So Worth It

❝ *We were having an in-class poetry slam and most of the kids did a great job, except for one girl. She was super-shy and refused to perform. I offered the whole class extra credit if they could get everyone to participate, and a bunch of kids rushed over to encourage her. At first I felt bad about putting her on the spot, but this class was full of nice kids who were very supportive. Finally, she realized she was going to get attention either way, so she stood up and read a poem. She got a ton of applause, and she looked so happy it made my day. As the year went on, she became less shy, and the following year, I saw her yelling in the hallway. I couldn't believe it was the same girl.* **❞**

MANIPULATIVE KIDS
Why They Will Infuriate You

Students who make up dead family members or switch classes for an easier grade will irritate you. Kids who excuse forty absences and then come in with makeup work on "report card eve" will make you want to whip ninja stars into their foreheads. Students who cheat the system also insult your intelligence and waste your time. After all, you're the one who has to grade that sloppy makeup work in time for report cards or pass that lazy student whose last five schools "lost" his transcripts.

> **❝** *I didn't know how much paperwork was involved in failing seniors. Teachers had to start a paper trail at least two months before graduation or the computer assigned a passing grade. One of my students knew this, and she stopped coming to class as soon as the deadline passed. By the time her grade dropped to an F, it was too late to do anything. She graduated with a C after skipping class for two months and even spread the word to my other students. Attendance was terrible the last three weeks of school.* **❞**

What They Need from You

Firm answers from the beginning   Except in the most extreme cases, start the year right by showing confidence in your grading system. Don't let kids talk you into changing grades. Don't let parents talk you into changing grades. Standing behind your decisions now will save lots of explaining later.

A paper trail   Make students sign for failure notices or excessive absences. Contact their parents and write it down. The more documentation you have, the better prepared you'll be to answer parents who "had no idea" their children were doing poorly.

A sharp eye for inconsistencies   If you suspect a student is scamming you, react carefully and slowly. Talk to his other teachers. Ask counselors to pull records. Listen to your gut feeling when something doesn't seem right, but do your homework before making accusations.

A wakeup call that sometimes you can't give them   If a student gets a free grade on a technicality or you lose a paperwork battle, do everything in your power to fix it. If you can't, take a deep breath and let it go. You learned your lesson, and you'll apply it with next year's class. They'll learn their own lesson when the time is right. Now go enjoy your summer.

Why You Shouldn't Let Them Make You Hate Your Job

" *One student that was a real pain was the student government president. I had her in a calculus class, so one might assume she was a decent student, but no. She was rude, lazy, manipulative, and downright ornery. She didn't study, didn't do homework, and generally thought I was going to give her a passing grade because it was her. I gave her a failure notice midway through the fourth nine weeks and told her to have a parent sign it. Of course, I made a copy with her signature. She never brought back the note, and she accused me of disrespectful language toward her. At the end of the year, she got her report card and sure enough, she had an F. Her mother called the school and demanded a conference in the principal's office. She accused me of keeping her daughter out of law school. This girl hadn't even spent one day in college, but she was already using me as her excuse for not getting into law school! The good news was I had done my job correctly. The principal backed me to the hilt. He refused to be bullied by the parent, and the failing grade stood. I didn't say it out loud, but if I was responsible for keeping that girl out of law school, I deserved a pat on the back.* **"**

BAD KIDS
Why You Will Sometimes Hate Them

Yes, I know. No kid is really "bad," and it's wrong to label kids. Unfortunately, right now you can't think of any other word to describe [insert name here]. Actually, you can think of lots of words...But let's just move on to the rest of the chapter.

"*I had one student who dominated my class. I had failed from square one in that I never set clear boundaries for his behavior. About two weeks into the year, he began…little by little…to get rowdier. Every time I reprimanded him, I never knew whether he was going to blow me off and put his head down or get mad and cuss at me in front of the class. He repeatedly said disrespectful things to his classmates, especially the girls. He constantly got off task, and he was failing the course content abysmally! I kept trying to recognize his improvement when he behaved well, but he always went back to his old ways. One day, a girl asked him an innocent question—something like 'Why were you late?' He cursed her out and tried to kick her. I was dismayed. He was the first student I ever wrote up. He spent most of the rest of that year serving in-school suspension for repeated behavioral offenses in multiple classes.***"*

What They Need from You

More attention   Teachers are often encouraged to use positive reinforcement with troublemakers, praising them for sample-sized
portions of good behavior. If you're like me, you find this mildly
offensive. These kids already waste more than their share of
your energy and class time. Now you have to treat them like
superheroes for not pushing in line? If a child's disruptions are
clearly cries for attention, though, you may be able to provide
this in other ways: make him responsible for a class job, offer
after-school tutoring, or pass by his desk frequently to check his
work. If all else fails, swallow your pride and compliment him
for not setting things on fire.

Less attention   Sometimes no amount of attention is enough to
keep a troublemaker from ruining your day, year, or general
mental health. If you sense this is the case, take a step in the
opposite direction. Start by moving her seat to a corner where
she's less likely to disturb the class. If necessary, turn her desk
toward the wall. Do your best to ignore misbehavior that is

simply irritating. You may find she calms down when she doesn't get the reaction she's hoping for.

Genuine concern Troublemakers often feel like teachers care less about them than the distractions they create. Sometimes they're right. When every bit of your feedback relates to a child's behavior, break that cycle by turning to a new subject. If you are so fed up that saying something nice would feel fake, force out a neutral comment, like "Zip your jacket so you don't get sick." Kids who feel you like them in spite of their actions may eventually begin to act in a way you like.

Accountability for their behavior It's tempting to create a double standard for an offender who just won't quit, but it's not recommended. Letting bad conduct slide paves the way for worse and shows the rest of your class that testing the rules pays off. It's also a disservice to the troublemakers themselves. Part of your job as a teacher is to help students develop social skills they will need later. Throwing tantrums is even less cute as an adult.

The benefit of the doubt...sometimes If your number-one perpetrator says she didn't do something, you didn't see it, and she rarely denies her offenses, she may be telling the truth. Your most frequent culprits aren't responsible for every problem, so try not to yell the same name every time something goes wrong. Chances are your instincts are right, but suppressing your blame reflex shows students you're willing to play fair.

What Their Classmates Need from You

When one student is so bad the rest of the class can't get an education, you need to balance his rights against those of everyone else. Sometimes you simply owe it to other students to remove this child from the class as quickly and as often as possible. In a functional school, this means writing referrals for every incident and following up until they are handled. If you know the office will dismiss your concerns or hold them against you, turn to a coworker you trust. They probably have experience with the situation, and they may have developed some solutions that don't depend on administrative support.

Why the Bad Days Are Often Worth It

"*My first day, one of my third-graders picked up on my inexperience and took control of the class. By the third day, he was hanging upside down in his seat. I spent all my energy on this kid's behavior, neglecting other students in the process. I called his house four times before calling any other parents. His grandmother came for a conference, but she couldn't even get him to sit down. I felt I was wasting my breath. Eventually, I started tutoring this student once a week after school. With no class to be a clown for, he became a nice kid. Slowly but surely his in-class behavior changed too. By the end of the year, his writing and behavior had both improved significantly. He turned out to be a wonderful student and a class leader in a good way. He also taught me a lesson I'm glad I learned early—don't give up on those 'nightmare kids.' They can become your most rewarding success stories.***"**

GOOD KIDS

We focus so much of our effort on getting kids to cooperate, participate, do their work, do it right, speak up, and sit down. The chaos of everyday teaching makes it easy to overlook students who do all these things automatically.

"*A new student transferred into my worst class. She did all her work, and it seemed like she was getting along fine with everyone. At that time, I used to give prizes at the end of the quarter for students who had not missed any***

assignments. This girl won first place, and another girl made a comment under her breath. I don't know what she said, but after that day, the girl completely stopped doing her work. She ended up failing the next semester. **99**

What They Need from You

The right kind of attention   Good kids reinforce the image we'd like to have of ourselves as teachers. When we're struggling with other students, it's tempting to look to them as proof of our success or hold them up as examples of what other kids could do if they "tried." Resist the urge to single out good kids as teacher's pets or put them in charge of getting classmates to behave. They may pay for it socially.

A challenge   Kids who are always a step ahead can end up bored, cocky, or eternally stuck in a "peer tutoring" role. You've heard of differentiated instruction, but the idea of planning a separate curriculum for one student probably makes you want to breathe into a paper bag. Instead, look for simpler ways to provide that extra push. Loan him books. Add complicated extra-credit problems to quizzes. If possible, recommend him for more advanced classes next year.

Why That Extra Push Pays Off

66 *I had one seventh-grader who knew every answer to every question and let his classmates know it. At one point, I even talked to him about toning it down so lower-level kids didn't feel bad. This student read any book I assigned in one night—he clearly belonged in a more advanced class. I started bringing high school-level and even a few college-level books that seemed to fit his interests. I also recommend him for honors classes the following year, and his eighth-grade teacher guided him into a selective high school that fit his talents. He seems very happy at his new school and still comes back to talk about books he has read.* **99**

HOW TO LIKE ALL YOUR KIDS BETTER

Part of our job is simply to be adults who care about kids. When we're frustrated with students' behavior or lack of effort, we sometimes forget there are other sides to their personalities and things going on in some of their lives that no kid should have to deal with. Students need to know teachers care about them whether or not they are "working to potential." Sometimes it takes a conscious effort to remind yourself that your students are human—and so are you.

1. Assign creative writing pieces that give them a chance to open up. Don't grade them hard, but read them as soon as possible.

2. Take pictures of students on field trips, at recess, or during free time in class. Kids seem much more lovable when you can look at them in silence. Post the pictures in your class so all of you have memories of the good times.

3. Cut up your class list and put the names in a box. Pick one name each morning and make an extra effort to pay attention to the child you picked.

4. Go to extracurricular events at your school and let students know you were there. If a student invites you to a family party, try to make an appearance. Seeing kids in a fresh environment shows you a different side of them, and shows them a different side of you.

All of the Above

by Roxanna Elden

I want my students to learn
To see the world with an open mind,
To read the fine print before they sign,

And not to believe everything they read,

But to read

Anyway.

Because when it's their turn to be heard,

I want them to have the right words to say.

I want them to stay tough

But still hold their own in a conversation

With anyone trying to judge them by their level
of education.

I want them to hold their own selves to the highest
expectations.

But this morning...

I'll just settle for some basic punctuation.

Because today I am hanging by the thinnest thread
of patience

I can find

And I'm grinding my teeth

To keep from losing my mind

Trying to find that little piece of genius

Buried under laziness

And make it shine,

Then find those magic words to make sure

"No child" gets "left behind,"

(Even when that child is rude, hardheaded,

Or even hard to find).

"Kids, maybe you can help me help you...any suggestions?"

"Uh...? Miss...? Do we have to write the questions?"

Am I teaching?

Or just preaching?

Making words come from my own mouth for my
own good

Yelling directions and deep thoughts deep in the
back woods

Thinking…

If none of my students hear me, do I even make
a sound?

Or am I just another teacher-tree falling on the
ground

Yelling teacher-lines as I flap my teacher branches
around?

But I *swear I thought we covered this much ground…*

NO!!!!!

I don't want you to copy the questions!

I want to know you are reading

And thinking,

I want to see that the horse that finally got to this
water is drinking.

Just let me know what I have to do

What I have to go through

To get through.

What concepts do I need to review?

(And document, of course,

For when the district comes through

But maybe that's my own anger management
issue…)

This job is not easy.

And students don't get it:

Adults work extra hard

Without extra credit.

And we know

We do whatever it takes...

Coming early, staying late

Snatching phones...calling homes...

Dealing with that combo

Of attitude and hormones...

Feeding dreams...

Coaching teams...

Bribing...yelling...

All while we review basic spelling...

And we feel like we failed

When kids don't care if they pass.

Some days, it's enough to make me want to cut
   my own class

Or at least ask:

What is it about all this that I say I love?

And I can't answer this

Until I pull out my class list,

Read it carefully

And circle,

"ALL OF THE ABOVE."

PARENTS: THE OTHER RESPONSIBLE ADULT

*M*ost parents at any school in any neighborhood want what is best for their children. The things teachers can do to form productive relationships with parents are usually simple.

While most parents will be helpful, however, this world is full of crazy people. Sometimes those people have kids, continue to act crazy, and become crazy parents. Your main relationship is with the child, but a parent on your side can make a huge difference, and a bad parent experience can ruin your day.

❝ *Parents don't realize how much more you hate their kid after they come in and confront you because they think you hate their kid. I had a mom who claimed I was plotting against her son and that's why he was failing. Her child had not turned in a single paper the whole year, and he came to class about twice a month—always with new gym shoes and brand-new clothes that his mommy bought him. He later went to prison. Apparently I wasn't the only one 'plotting' against him.* ❞

❝ *I called the home of a student who had many unexcused absences. Her mother requested a conference after school the following week. Then she missed the conference and never called to offer an excuse for her own absence.* ❞

"*A parent walked into my class and started yelling at me. I didn't want to have the conversation in front of my class, so I stepped outside. She got in my face and backed me up against the lockers and started cursing and threatening me until other teachers came out of their classrooms and someone called the office for help.***"**

"*I had one mother who had been a teacher herself and told me my job was easy. She didn't mention why she had stopped teaching.***"**

"*A parent called my house and called me all kinds of names because her daughter wasn't doing well. She blamed me for the fact that her child hadn't shown her a progress report or report card all semester.***"**

"*A student in an honors class filed some papers he had never turned in and put grades on them. His mother said he would never do this and never lie. We all had a conference with the assistant principal. It was never resolved, but I believe his mother really knew the truth.***"**

"*There was a young man in my fourth-period English class who thought since we were both Jamaican, I would let his bad behavior slide. I had done an excellent job of ignoring his profane language, pornographic conversations, and explicit cartoons passed around the classroom, but I could not ignore his lighting a piece of rolled paper and offering it as 'crack' to another classmate. Although he did nothing in class, this student was smart. The one piece of written work he turned in that year was brilliant, so I was not surprised at his mother's vocabulary when she wrote a nasty e-mail about the referral I submitted for her son, including several references from our shared culture. I thought of many colorful responses to this woman. Instead, I decided to take the e-mail and the referral to the appropriate assistant principal. I asked him to apply his years of experience to the matter, as I did not think the solutions in my head would result in me keeping my job. He did. So here I am.***"**

❝ *One father accused me of 'talking out of both sides of my mouth.' I had spoken with him a week earlier because his son was failing the class and behaving horribly. The kid's behavior improved, so I called home again, hoping this would encourage him. The father asked if his son was still failing, and when I said yes, he called me a hypocrite for calling with good news. No more positive parent contact for him…* **❞**

❝ *I actually did not have any difficult parents. Most of the parents were—to my biased surprise—ready and willing to help me help their children. One mother was so incensed when I told her that her son had cheated on an exam, she actually called him over and started to hit him while she was still on the phone with me. I felt so bad. I tried to calm her down, but she was pretty heated. I believe that student made it out okay, though. He's in college today!* **❞**

❝ *On the evening of my school's open house, other teachers warned me about parents having attitudes or trying to force me into detailed conferences. They told me to keep it short. But the parents of my ESL students were not the type I was warned about. None of the parents who came that night would ever throw open the door to my classroom and yell at me, or demand a grade change from the principal. Very few people in the school spoke Spanish, and these parents were not used to being heard. No one asked me to go out of my way at all, but something in their eyes said, 'Please be a good teacher. Please educate my child right.' It was a look I could not meet directly yet. A promise I could not make. I kept it short, like the other teachers said.* **❞**

TIPS FOR DEALING WITH PARENTS IN GENERAL

Get in touch as early as possible. Teachers who introduce themselves to parents early say it sets the tone for the whole year. If you are too overwhelmed to do this, you can forgive yourself. Just don't lose your credibility with students by telling them you will call home if you are too busy to keep the promise.

Assume the best. Parents are your allies in most cases. It is safe to assume that parents have the best interest—or what they think is the best interest—of their child in mind. Even if you don't understand their actions or reactions to you, give them credit for good intentions. Few people want their kids to be failures.

Be respectful. This is probably common sense, but you will never get a better attitude from a parent than you give.

Be honest. One piece of advice offered as common sense is to feed parents a "compliment sandwich." This means starting and ending negative phone calls with positive comments about the child. When appropriate, starting a call with good news shows parents you don't hate their children or consider them hopeless. In other cases, diluting complaints with compliments can make you sound weak or hypocritical—and toning down a serious offense is just silly. Some teacher phone calls *should* make parents feel horrified. One way to show concern without seeming fake is to say you've noticed a change in the student's behavior ("She has never acted like this before, so I'm wondering if something is bothering her"). You can also say something positive about the parents if you have dealt with them before, like "I don't know what you said to him last time we spoke, but I definitely noticed a change in his attitude." Then drop the news about the newest problem.

Write it down. Every time you talk to parents, write down the date, the purpose of the call, and a one-sentence summary of the discussion. Keep these sheets in students' record folders and pull them out before the next call or meeting. These records remind you of past conversations and prove you have made contact.

Listen. Sometimes there are valid reasons why students don't work or behave as well as we want them to. Parents may provide eye-opening facts that can help you work better with their children.

SPECIAL TIPS FOR ESPECIALLY DIFFICULT PARENTS

Have proof. Get kids to sign for any form you send home. Keep letters, notes, homework…anything that proves a point you may need to make later. This arms you if you have to take disciplinary action or give a failing grade. Walking into a conference with a folder full of evidence is a great confidence booster, and it can quickly change the tone of parents who have been taking their children's word over yours.

Have someone else around. If you think that a parent may get out of line or lie about something you said, don't meet alone. Have an administrator, another teacher, or even a security guard sit down with you.

Keep detailed records. You should always document parent contact, but if you think a parent will cause future problems, write conversations in more detail. You don't need to overdo this—just make sure you can clearly remember your side of the story.

Keep your cool. No matter how mad parents make you, remember that you are the professional. They won't have to explain their actions to your boss. You might. They will be gone next year. You don't want to be.

THE TEACHERS' LOUNGE: MAKING IT WORK WITH THE PEOPLE YOU WORK WITH

THINGS NEVER TO SAY IN THE TEACHERS' LOUNGE

Before my first year, a veteran teacher warned me to stay out of the teachers' lounge. She said it would be full of negative teachers gossiping about kids, coworkers, and probably me as soon as I left the room. This turned out to be easy advice to follow. I spent every lunch period in my classroom giving "lunch detentions," staring at ungraded papers, or hyperventilating in the dark. At the end of the year, I regretted it. Getting to know your coworkers makes any job more enjoyable, and we all need to socialize sometimes. Why do you think it's so hard to keep the kids quiet?

My second year, I made sure to eat lunch in the lounge at least once a week, and it wasn't as bad as everyone said. Okay, I'm lying. It was exactly like everyone said, but it was still better than spending the whole day without seeing other adults. I also got to catch up on some good gossip.

Over time, you can find the right balance between company and privacy, but there's one guarantee at any school: everyone talks to someone, and someone in the teachers' lounge talks to *everyone*. Schools are filled with complex office politics that you won't figure out until well after your first year. With that in mind, here are a few examples of things not to share:

- "I'm so hungover."
- "I hate working here."
- "I can't control my class's behavior."
- "The teacher next door to me can't control her class."
- "This job is easy for me. My kids said they never learned as much with any other teacher."
- "Did you know that fat kid's mom is a lesbian?"
- "I keep staring at our principal's wig while she's talking."

The general rule is that if there is anything you wouldn't want repeated to a coworker, overheard by your principal, or announced out of context over the PA system, the teachers' lounge is not the place to discuss it.

DIFFICULT COWORKERS

Many of your coworkers will be outstanding citizens…or at least smart, nice people who genuinely care about kids. At every school, however, there are a few reminders that you don't need a license to carry a "#1 Teacher!!!" mug. Here are a few warnings about who might be roaming your hallway.

Other New Teachers Who Won't Stop Bragging

While being a rookie teacher is hard for most of us, some teachers claim to have everything together from the first day. Their students "know who's in charge," "never miss class," and "are finally learning that school can be a positive experience." They never struggle with parents or paperwork. In fact, these superstars have solved problems experienced teachers still encounter—and all in the first few weeks! It goes without saying they have already thought of *your* best ideas.

❝*I taught a low-level class with thirty-four students. Two brilliant boys had been stuck in this class for years because no one had looked at their files. I filled out the paperwork to switch them to a gifted class, also taught by a beginning teacher. A few weeks later, the teacher made a point to tell me one of the students said he was learning more in her class than he had in mine. Thanks for the update! She had a class of eighteen and taught only two subjects, and she still complained regularly. I wish we could have switched for a week.***❞**

❝*I had to switch classrooms with another new teacher in the middle of the school year. My old room didn't have air-conditioning, and this was in a hot climate with about thirty teenagers in each room. The first thing this teacher said was 'Your room smells musty. Mine smells nice.' This was not her first obnoxious comment. Needless to say, I didn't mind giving her the room without air-conditioning.***❞**

❝*Another rookie teacher who taught the same grade I did seemed to have nothing but success stories. We met a few times to plan lessons together, but he often interrupted to have loud, optimistic conversations with parents. We never got around to planning any lessons, and I always left these sessions feeling depressed and inadequate. At the end of the year, I visited my former planning buddy's summer school class, hoping to unlock the secret to his success. The secret was...he wasn't that successful. Don't get me wrong—he worked hard and had some good ideas. However, he also had students who didn't understand a word of his lessons and others who were openly disrespectful. In other words, his class was a lot like mine. I have visited many other classrooms since and have seen some amazing teachers, but I've seen very little correlation between bragging and excellent teaching.***❞**

How to Deal with Teachers Who Brag

- Don't ask them for advice or admit weaknesses in front of them. They are likely to repeat your problems to make themselves look better.

- Don't try to get them to admit their weaknesses. They won't. With time, though, questions may float to the surface.

- Remember that there is a macho element to being a new teacher, especially for people who believe they must be good at everything right away. In many cases, rookies who claim to have it all under control are secretly reassuring themselves.

- If you can stand it, listen anyway. They may have some good ideas.

- If a coworker's self-promotions start getting on your nerves, smile, nod, and find an excuse to leave the room.

How to Make Sure This Isn't *Your* Reputation

- If you can't offer encouragement to distraught coworkers, at least offer silence. Resist the urge to "inspire" them with chicken-soup-type stories from your own day. Talking about your most recent achievements is actually a sucker punch to their souls and will make them feel lower than they already do.

- If another teacher offers you well-meaning advice, say "Thank you," even if you already knew it. You don't need to prove you know too much to hear advice. You need to prove you know enough to listen to it.

- If your principal makes positive comments during an observation, share them with your mentor teacher or a non-teacher friend, not the struggling rookie next door.

- Remember that other teachers may have harder jobs, even at the same school. This is especially true if you teach high-level students or a class that lets you escape test pressure.

- Don't encourage kids to badmouth other teachers. If they do, don't repeat it.

- Remember it is rare for more experienced teachers to see rookies as role models. Many new teachers are full of ideas and willing to put in long hours, but your coworkers have also established routines they can keep up year after year. You haven't yet, and you will show good judgment by remembering to be humble.
- Never assume you are the only competent or hardworking person in your school. You're not.

Negative Teachers

Complaining about your job is a lot like drinking. A little bit, around the right people, can be just what you need. If you do it too much, though, you'll be sorry. You often feel guilty and emotionally drained afterward, and if you do it in the wrong company, you can damage your reputation.

Also, as with drinking, some people just can't seem to stop complaining. Negative colleagues can be other rookies who want to know they're not alone or disillusioned veterans who think they're doing you a favor. Sometimes their complaints feel refreshingly honest. Too much time in the company of complainers, however, can leave you feeling hopeless. It's nice to have sympathy after a bad day, but you need to feel your job is still possible and worthwhile. Otherwise, why are you doing it?

❝ *There was a teacher who would constantly talk about my seventh-graders in front of her sixth-graders. She wouldn't mention names, but she would point to my class list and say things like 'I had this girl last year and now I have her sister. The sister is smart, but the one you have is as dumb as a box of rocks.' She didn't think she was being obvious, but the details she gave were enough for students to figure out who she was talking about. I would see them looking up while they pretended to be working. I could never end those conversations fast enough.* **❞**

❝For me, being a role model means having integrity, working hard, being respectful, and acting professional. Sometimes I feel like the actions of other teachers at my school don't really align with those values. There are teachers who complain about their salaries to the kids, who curse at students, or who don't take a lot of time to make class meaningful. This is frustrating because it perpetuates a culture of low expectations that hurts my students' self-esteem and desire to succeed. I think some of the burned-out teachers struggle so much to have a positive attitude about students. Lots of times, the negative things they say show their frustration from years of attempting to overcome obstacles and failing to a certain degree.**❞**

How to Deal with Negative Teachers

- Listen. If you want to know your school's dirty secrets, a fed-up veteran is your best source.
- Think twice before jumping in with your own stories. You don't want this person using them as examples next time they complain.
- Don't push complainers too hard to see the bright side. They may just write you off as naive or conceited.
- Understand where they're coming from. There are reasons a twenty-year veteran teacher may have gotten cynical.
- If the person starts to depress you, smile, nod, and find a reason to leave the room.

How to Make Sure This Isn't *Your* Reputation

- Be careful whom you talk to after a bad day.
- Watch what you discuss in front of students. Any students.
- Understand that complaining only helps in moderation. If you are constantly complaining and never quite get it out of your system, you are probably dragging yourself down without realizing it.
- Find a hobby that doesn't involve talking about your job or, better yet, that takes your mind off it completely.

- If other people smile, nod, and leave the room when you start a sentence with "These kids…," you may want to lighten up a little bit.

Coworkers Who Don't Do Their Jobs and Make Yours Harder

Part of our job as teachers is to set an example for students, so it's frustrating to see incompetent, lazy, and dishonest people infiltrating the school system. Even worse, some have found a permanent home in your school at the expense of hardworking teachers and all students.

"*I sometimes get annoyed at teachers who come in my class and talk endlessly when I'm trying to plan. Then I get angry when the same teachers want me to give them work for the students because they didn't prepare. I believe in sharing, but not pulling someone else's weight.***"**

"*The school's reading specialist came to help get my third-graders ready for the state test. This woman was a veteran teacher with several degrees under her belt, but she told my class the proper pronunciation of the word mammal was man-uh-mal. I almost died. The woman was old enough to be my mother, and I felt uncomfortable telling her how to pronounce mammal. However, I couldn't let my students grow up thinking the word rhymed with animal. I decided to do a lesson on syllables the next day, and make sure we clapped out mam-mal along with other vocabulary words. Thankfully, all my students learned the proper pronunciation!***"**

"*The counselor at our school took on every responsibility that would add to her paycheck, including the special ed and ESL departments. Then she took extra-long lunch breaks and got manicures during school hours. Meanwhile, the kids' needs were ignored. Their folders were filled with forged signatures. Students waited years for special services or sat in ESL classes even though they spoke perfect English. This woman was the principal's best friend. Teachers had to explain delays to angry parents without getting her in trouble.***"**

How to Deal with Teachers or Faculty Who Don't Do Their Jobs

- Pick your battles. If no one is in danger, you probably don't want to take on this case your first year. Your principal may have been trying to get rid of this person for years. Or your principal may be related to this person. Leave time for the facts to come out before facing off with a lazy coworker.
- If you are asked to cover for someone else's irresponsibility in a way that weighs on your conscience or gets you in trouble, refuse. This person will surely be out of sight when it's time to answer questions.

How to Make Sure This Isn't *Your* Reputation

- Return favors and borrowed supplies as soon as possible.
- Get teaching advice from people you trust not to repeat your concerns. If you get the feeling your questions are being used against you, confide in a teacher who doesn't work with you.
- Avoid comments about what you are "not contractually obligated" to do. Unions have fought hard to keep teachers from being abused, but most of us still work many more hours than our contracts require.

Other Teachers Who Won't Give You a Chance Because of Something You Can't Control, Who Have No Social Skills, or Who Are Just Rude, Mean-Spirited, Nasty, Horrendous People Who Don't Make the Earth a Better Place

"*I was hired to teach an honors class another teacher wanted. Even though it obviously wasn't my decision, she took it out on me in little ways the entire year, gave me the silent treatment, and talked about me behind my back. She got married that year and invited every teacher in my department except me. She even passed out some of the invitations in front of my face.***"**

66 *I had an overflow class of kids who had been kicked out of other schools or whose parents had forgotten to sign them up on time. Almost all of them were behavior problems. My coworkers knew I was having a rough year, and most were helpful and encouraging, but one day I was called for a conference and the media specialist had to cover my class. The kids were behaving when she walked in, but when I started to tell her what she could do if there was a problem, she cut me off. She said, 'Don't worry. They won't give me any problems.' Then she turned to the kids and yelled, 'I am not your regular teacher and I am not white. You will not run me around like you do her.' Besides being unnecessarily racist, this turned out not to be much of a discipline plan. When I came back an hour later, she had already sent two of the kids to the office. She said, 'These kids are bad!'* **99**

How to Deal with Horrendous Bitches and Unapologetic Assholes

- Don't let the actions of a few outspoken, ignorant people keep you from getting to know your other coworkers. The more allies you have, the less one person's attitude matters.

- Be patient. The more chaotic your school, the more likely it is to be a revolving door for well-intentioned new teachers. Try not to take it personally if some coworkers treat you like you won't be around next year. They will take you more seriously once you've proven your staying power, and you will have seen enough teachers quit to understand their skepticism.

- When deciding how to handle difficult coworkers, consider your own personality and your relationship with the person in question. In some cases, standing up for yourself prevents people from bullying you in the future. Other times it's better to let an incident slide than take on a new enemy. This is a call you need to make for yourself.

How to Make Sure This Isn't *Your* Reputation

- If you've read this far, you're probably okay. Those who are truly at risk aren't worried about whether they fall into this category; they are much too busy stealing parking spots from cars with elderly passengers and pulling the whiskers off baby bunnies.

A NOTE ABOUT MENTOR TEACHERS

Many contributors to this book cited mentors as their lifelines. Mentor teachers get small stipends for taking beginners under their wings, but the majority of them chose the responsibility because they remember the trials they faced as rookies and want good teachers at their schools. Mentors can give some of those tips you didn't learn in education classes. They are usually happy to help.

In unlucky cases, your principal has different things in mind when picking your mentor than you would. If your mentor got the position by being the principal's best friend, next in line, or next door to your classroom, you may end up with someone whose main job is to report your mistakes. If this is the case, it's time to start looking for an unofficial mentor generous enough to answer your questions for free.

If you were lucky enough, like I was (thanks, Mrs. Orr), to be assigned an outstanding teacher who is also a wonderful mentor, be thankful. Still, keep the following tips in mind:

- **Your mentor teacher probably gets paid to be a mentor.** Don't be shy about scheduling meetings and asking job-related questions.
- **Your mentor teacher doesn't get paid much to be a mentor.** Other teachers in your school have as many papers to grade and lessons to plan as you do. Don't use up mentors' energy and goodwill by expecting them to do your job for you.
- **Keep your opinions about your principal and colleagues to yourself.** Unless a person is causing you serious problems and you are confident of

your mentor's discretion, don't share anything you wouldn't say in the teachers' lounge. Your mentor has been assigned to help you, but has known these people for years and needs to work with them for years to come.

- **If you don't think your mentor is a great teacher, keep an open mind.** Your first impression may be wrong, and even if it's right, you can learn a few things.
- **You may not teach the same subject, grade, or skill level as your mentor.** If this person can't provide all the answers you need, reach out to other coworkers in your department.
- **Get to know as many teachers as you can and be open to their advice.** Sometimes your greatest mentor is not the one assigned by your principal.

13
PLEASE REPORT TO THE PRINCIPAL'S OFFICE

*I*n college, students are encouraged to share their opinions, keep debates lively, and play the devil's advocate. You have likely noticed this is not the case at your school's faculty meetings. School meetings tend to be top-down affairs: administrators deliver information from the front of the cafeteria or auditorium while teachers sit silently on the receiving end. Should you try to change this dynamic? Should you be the one to speak out? Should you lead the way in challenging high-level decisions, thus taking a stand for your educational beliefs and proving to administrators and colleagues alike that even new teachers deserve a place at the decision-making table?

Probably not.

One of the most common mistakes new teachers make is crossing administrative radar too early, too often, and for the wrong reasons. As a new teacher, you haven't had time to earn much credibility. You may even make a few mistakes yourself this year and need some good will from administrators, which makes it extra important to choose your battles carefully. Your best bet as a beginner is to stay quiet and attentive during faculty meetings and keep comments about your principal's competence, personality, and hairstyle to yourself.

It's not always easy.

THINGS ADMINISTRATORS DO THAT DRIVE TEACHERS CRAZY
Act Hypocritically

"*An assistant principal asked me to smoke pot with him at my first faculty holiday party. From that time until I left the school, I found it very difficult to work with him. I was so disappointed in this person who should have been a role model. Years later, I taught his niece at another school. He made a point to see me and ask me not to mention the incident to her.***"**

"*At the beginning of the year, an older kid who was not enrolled in the school came into my freshman class regularly. He turned off the lights, wrote curse words on the blackboard, and once dumped my trash can onto the floor. No one knew who this kid was. I pressed the emergency button whenever he came in, but never received an answer, and there was no security guard assigned to my hallway. My assistant principal never answered any of the referrals I wrote about the situation. Several months later, the same assistant principal walked past my classroom during a group activity. He noticed it was noisy and began asking me regularly whether I was okay and if I had problems controlling my class.***"**

Ignore School Discipline

"*Our assistant principal talks to behavior problems for one minute and returns them to the classroom immediately. Sometimes they come back laughing. It's infuriating.***"**

"*Our principal wanted to keep attendance numbers high, so she often reversed our assistant principal's decisions to suspend kids. In one case, a third-grader punched a pregnant teacher in the stomach and was back at school the following day. The principal got a $5,000 bonus at the end of the year for improving our attendance numbers.***"**

Play Favorites

" *We had a principal who would undermine teachers' authority and criticize them behind their backs to other teachers. In one incident, a parent made a need-less, insulting comment about a teacher and she agreed.* **"**

" *Our principal hired a bunch of her friends to work at the school. Some were good teachers, but others were ridiculous hiring decisions by any standard. To make things worse, she never observed any of these people. She also let them adjust their class lists and move their worst students to other teachers.* **"**

Waste Teachers' Time

" *My old principal had meetings every single morning. Some of the meetings had no agenda, and he would just talk until the bell rang. It was like he was afraid of what we would do if he left us alone in our classrooms during our free time.* **"**

" *We had this one guy who thought it was a good idea to get on the intercom at the beginning of every period and tell students which class they were supposed to be in. Then he would wait until a few minutes after the bell, when we were already teaching, and interrupt to give kids what he thought was an encouraging pep talk. He would sometimes use the last ten minutes of class to continue these speeches. For years, he spent about twenty minutes of each day on the intercom. The saddest part was no one listened. Acoustics in the school were so bad the messages were garbled anyway.* **"**

Notice Only the Bad Things

" *Our school had lots of students who loved soccer and weren't involved in other activities. I asked if I could start a soccer team. My principal told me to write a proposal then lost three copies of it in three weeks. Her disorganization* *combined with her need to control everything made every step harder than it needed to be. By the time I brought her the paperwork, forms, and letters I had typed, it was clear I'd put in many hours outside of school. I'm not sure what I expected from her at that point, but I think I was hoping for some encouragement. Instead, she skimmed all six papers, found a typo in one of them, and said, 'You're going to fix this before you make copies, right?'* **"**

"*I had a deal with one of my hyperactive students: if he behaved well in the morning, he got to sit on his desk during story time. My principal passed by the room and saw this. She came in to yell at the student. Then she reprimanded me for bad classroom management, even though all the kids had been listening silently when she walked in. At the next faculty meeting, she made an announcement about classes being out of control and 'kids climbing on the furniture.'* **"**

Ignore the Effects of Their Decisions

"*One administrator decided to observe me during open house my first year. Talk about nerve-racking. Another assistant principal made me come to his office in the middle of a midterm to talk to a parent. My class took the whole test alone while a security officer looked in from the hallway.* **"**

"*A second-grader went home with a chunk of her hair cut off, and her mom called the school. Our principal's reaction was to get on the PA and demand that every teacher stop class, have the kids look through their desks for scissors, and then lock up all the scissors for the rest of the year. According to the announcement, we were supposed to give back all the scissors on the last day of school. Great! Let's take a day when lots of fights start and give every child a sharp object to take home! On top of this, the announcement sounded so frantic that students started asking if someone got murdered. It turned out the girl had cut her own hair and told her mom it was another student so she wouldn't get in trouble.* **"**

Bully and Harass Teachers

66 *Our district had a hiring freeze in place, and I was on a temporary contract. My principal said she didn't know if she would get authorization to rehire me. I called the school every week all summer. No one would tell me anything or return my calls. Finally, less than one week before school started, I got an offer from another school. Of course I took it. My principal called me the next day and said, 'Congratulations, you have your job back.' When I told her I got another job, she called me a 'fucking little baby' and said, 'You will work here.' Needless to say, I didn't want to work for her anyway at that point, and I went to human resources freaking out. They told me not to worry because she didn't really have the power to keep me from switching schools.* 99

66 *Everyone at our school has at least one story about our principal embarrassing them, yelling at them in front of students, calling them out in meetings, or making out-of-line comments. Once I went into her office to ask about some supplies I had requested several times. She interrupted me, yelled at me for a few minutes, and then waved me out of the office before I could answer. I was so furious that tears came to my eyes. Another teacher offered to watch my kids so I could run to the bathroom and cool off. She said, 'Don't worry. We've all been there.' Over time, the resentment toward our principal has built up and taken its toll on staff morale. We've lost several good teachers because of it.* 99

Make Important Changes at the Last Minute

66 *Our principal spent thousands of dollars on a school-wide reading program. He sent us all for training, where we learned that if the program was not implemented school-wide, every day, it would not work. We received materials so we could each do our part. At the meeting about how to implement the program, one teacher complained, and the principal backed down and said, 'Well, just do it in your own classes if you think it's a good idea.' A few teachers tried to cooperate*

and make it work, but, like the training said, it had to be a school-wide effort. Within one week, we all gave up. All those boxes of workbooks just sat there collecting dust. **99**

66 *One month into the year, administrators told us our schedules might change completely—apparently we were out of compliance with some district non-sense. As if that weren't enough, they couldn't tell us for sure, so we spent two months not knowing if students would stay in our classes. Then we came in one Monday and found out we were switching the following day. We spent the rest of the week trying to set a serious tone with the whole school in a state of confusion. New kids trickled into our classrooms while old students poked their heads in, not knowing where to go.* **99**

Discipline Teachers Instead of Students

66 *One day, two girls in my advanced class were audibly arguing, for the simple fact that they didn't like each other. Making a rookie mistake, I told the girls to be quiet and save the fighting until they got out of my classroom. Each rolled their eyes at the other but kept quiet. Immediately following dismissal, the two students stepped out of the classroom and began to fight their way down the hallway. They were taken to the vice principal's office and repeated my misspoken words. This particular vice principal was all about disciplining teachers and not students. They were her 'babies,' as she affectionately called them. The girls walked away with no punishment, which I had expected. What did surprise me was when one of the student's mothers came to my classroom to tell me the vice principal had suggested she complain to the district about my incompetence. She said that I had actually encouraged the children to fight, and the parent had to stand up to her on my behalf. I learned two lessons that day: be good to your classroom parents, and, if you don't have the principal's support, you definitely have to watch your back!* **99**

IN DEFENSE OF ALL PRINCIPALS—EVEN YOURS

Running a school is hard, and principals face their own challenges in the school system's chain of command. They deliver bad news to their bosses, relay district decisions to employees, and field complaints at both ends. They are also the most visible targets when school problems gain public attention. Yes, wonderful principals have turned schools around. Yes, we sometimes imagine what it might be like to work for Joe Clark, the inspiring hero of *Lean on Me,* who fought back against the system and patrolled the halls of his troubled high school with a bat and a bullhorn while still making time to share encouraging, emotional moments with teachers and students. At the same time, no one knows better than we do how frustrating it is to be compared to the movie version of our job. It is unfair to assume all problems begin and end with your front office.

YOUR PRINCIPAL VS. YOUR PRINCIPLES: HOW TO SPEAK UP WHEN YOU REALLY NEED TO

Your administration is like a bra: if it offers the support you need, you both look and feel better. If it fits poorly, it can get in your way and even become painful. This makes it understandably scary when you have to approach your principal directly, but a tough conversation doesn't have to mean making enemies in the main office. Walk in with the following tips in mind, and you are more likely to walk out happy.

- **Pick the right moment.** Certain times of day or year are tense for administrators. If your boss is handling an emergency, district supervisors are in the building, or a high-stakes test is next week, it's a bad time to knock on the door to follow up on a discipline referral.

- **Pick one issue at a time.** Your principal is more likely to listen to your request to replace broken desks if it's not combined with an unrelated complaint about the lunch schedule. Focus on your highest priority and leave other topics for another day.

- **Offer a solution.** Administrators have the same problem with overwhelming to-do lists that teachers do. Your principal will be more receptive if you approach with a plan of action you'd like her to sign off on rather than a problem you hope she will figure out how to solve.

- **Offer to do most of the work.** When someone is trying to sell you a car or a gym membership, they handle the paperwork themselves. All you have to do is say yes and sign. Keep this model in mind when you want your principal to approve your field trip request. If you get the answer you want, expect to make phone calls, fill out paperwork, and collect permission slips on your own.

- **Keep it to a minimum.** Before crossing an administrator's radar, consider your own scorecard. Did your principal have to calm down angry parents last week? Have you just requested a schedule change or ordered expensive supplies? Have you been writing lots of referrals? If so, give it some time. Requests and complaints can combine with other issues to make you seem like a high-maintenance employee.

- **Keep it private.** We often hear that students need to save face and will react badly if confronted in public. This advice applies to people of any age, and it definitely applies to your boss. Don't embarrass your principal—or yourself—by airing private complaints in public.

- **Keep records.** Maintain a "professional responsibilities" file with copies of paperwork you've turned in to the main office. Make notes on any discussion that could relate to your future employment. If you believe you'll want proof of a conversation with an administrator, try to have that conversation by email. Just remember that email is a record for both parties. Proofread carefully before you hit "send," and never write work-related emails when you are mad.

- **Be professional.** If talking to your boss makes you feel like you're stuck in a *Dilbert* cartoon, try not to let it show. Trying to change a supervisor's management style or IQ won't help anyway, and losing your cool could hurt your career.
- **Be realistic.** It's usually not worth heading to the main office with matters outside your administration's control. School-level administrators aren't in charge of every decision, and there is a limit to the number of times your principal can approach higher ups with requests or grievances. Principals need to stay on their boss's good sides too.

WHAT YOUR PRINCIPAL REALLY WANTS FROM YOU

What most principals want from teachers is simple and matches what any boss wants from employees:

- Do your job.
- Do your job well.
- Do your job as independently and with as little drama as possible.
- Make yourself, your students, the school, and, yes, your principal look as good as possible.

The good news is that no matter what you think of your boss, experienced teachers agree that when you close the classroom door, your students are in your world. They work for you. You work for them.

Memo
by Erica Elden

Attention all teachers
Please cancel all teaching or learning you had
   planned for today

We need some data.

Administer these diagnostic tests.

Ensure all students take them seriously.

Ignore all comments of "We have to read *all four* pages!?"

Do not allow talking, cheating, or sleeping.

You say you already know your kids can't read this?

You say you know it will make them feel bored, frustrated,

Like school is a waste of their time?

Oh…well, we need proof of their failure for our database.

Diagnostic tests must be graded by Friday.

Attached is one diagnostic test.

Please photocopy.

14
STRESSIN' ABOUT LESSONS

❝ *I borrowed a peer-editing idea from a colleague and planned it into my writing lesson: students were to number their papers one through twelve, then find partners for each number and write their names on one another's papers on the same number. Each time we needed to peer edit throughout the year, I planned to roll a giant pair of dice. The number that came up would dictate which partner students would work with that day. It sounded like a great way to keep my students from always working with the same person. It also sounded like a simple enough idea to explain to high school students. It was not. Every time we switched to a new number, there was a new issue. 'I don't have a partner.' 'Oops, I wrote my name on the wrong number on a few people's papers.' 'Yay, I have my whole paper filled up before anyone else in the class! Oh, I was supposed to sign the other person's paper too?' After several false starts, we finally got everyone paired off correctly and actually got to peer edit for the last few minutes of class. The next time I tried to use the system, though, we had a new round of problems. 'My partner isn't here.' 'I lost my paper.' 'Hey, you rolled that number last time! We're all working with the same person anyway.'* **❞**

❝ *I tried to draw the state of Florida on the board, and my eighth-graders kept laughing. When I stepped back I saw why—the drawing looked like a four-foot penis. Oops.* **❞**

“*I had attended a workshop and learned a trick for teaching vocabulary—a word map shaped like a teddy bear. The idea was to put the word on the bear's head, the definition on the stomach, et cetera. Kids were supposed to make one word bear each day and study them during their free time. I couldn't wait to share this idea with my third-graders. What I didn't realize was that (a) a teddy bear is a hard thing for eight-year-olds to draw, and (b) third-graders are way more interested in drawing a good teddy bear than creating a useful word map. The point of the activity was completely lost. Also, what took ten minutes in the workshop took over an hour in my class. I figured it would go faster the second day, but somehow it took even longer. There was no third day.***”***

“*Many lessons have fallen victim to school-wide events that cause students to miss class. The problem is at its worst in the last two months of the year, when our school does computer-based testing. The only way to accommodate all students is to schedule testing so about one third of students miss class at any given time. This means there are at least ten students every class who missed the previous lesson, but also at least ten students who would be bored out of their minds if I tried to reuse the same lesson plan.***”***

COMMON LESSON ROADBLOCKS

Let's assume you know it's important to come to school prepared with a lesson plan. Let's even assume you've learned the five-part lesson format and spend many hours at home planning detailed lessons with hooks, direct instruction, guided and independent practice, and closing activities that allow for assessment of student learning. Those hoping to set high standards are quick to emphasize the importance of good lesson plans. Sometimes, however, they forget to mention that lessons can look great on paper and still play out horribly in the classroom. Here are some of the more common reasons good lessons go bad.

1. **Kids don't have the background knowledge you thought they did.** You introduce your Black History Month essay topic: "Has Dr. Martin Luther King Jr.'s dream for America come true?" You get nothing but blank stares. You ask what the kids know about Dr. King, and the answers include "He was president" and "He freed the slaves." The good news is you know what you'll be teaching today. The bad news is everything else.

2. **A "teachable moment" gets you off track and off schedule.** Some of your best lessons will come from moments that let you push aside your plans and discuss something that fascinates students. Use these moments to your advantage. Just be careful not to turn every teachable moment into a "teachable day" or a "let-me-tell-you-my-life-story" moment. When the kids start looking bored, the moment has probably passed. Also, keep in mind that teachable moments still involve topics that don't reveal too much of your personal life. Questions such as "How was your weekend?" are *not* questions that lead to teachable moments. Also keep in mind that much depends on context. Questions such as "Is oral sex really sex?" may lead to a valuable teachable moment if you are teaching health or human anatomy, but probably not if you are teaching advanced calculus.

3. **Your kids already did your fraction-pizza lesson with their last teacher.** It seemed original while you were cutting out circles of colored foam, gluing them together, tracking down enough scissors for twenty-seven tiny hands, and writing directions on the board in advance. Then your little angels come in and say, "Man, we're doing fraction pizzas *again*?" Guess what, kids? This is review!

4. **You explained the directions, but the kids have no idea what you're talking about.** Over time, you will learn to give clearer directions and break tasks into the appropriate number of smaller steps. The first time you run into this problem, though, you have

two choices: backtrack and walk students through every step or simplify the assignment. If you backtrack, you'll probably spend longer on the activity than you planned. Simplifying cuts your losses, but the kids may not get everything you wanted out of the activity. Either way, you get a lesson in thinking on your feet. Hey, at least someone's learning.

5. **The projector breaks, the copies aren't made, or you can't find the workbooks.** It's always a good idea to double-check your materials and have extra supplies on hand, but no one needs to tell you that right now. The good news is there are often ways to work around missing materials, even if it means dictating questions while students write them down. Think one-room schoolhouse. If that doesn't work, use tomorrow's plans or switch to a review activity.

6. **You realize your lesson is going to end early.** One of the worst feelings as a new teacher is when a lesson ends earlier than expected. You see the kids finishing their assignment. You look at the clock. There are thirty minutes of class left, which in no-lesson-plan time is like a week and a half. You start hoping there's an announcement, a fire drill, a real fire—anything to keep you from having to answer the dreaded question, "So what are we doing next?"

SO WHAT *ARE* WE DOING NEXT?

Let me be the first to say that none of the following suggestions replaces real teaching. Think of them as emergency substitute plans for yourself. Their purpose is to provide productive crowd control in an emergency or keep leftover minutes from turning into a classroom management nightmare.

- Make extra copies of activities kids can do on their own. Keep these in a place where students can find them if they finish early.

- If you teach in a self-contained classroom, have students keep "I'm Done" folders in their desks. These can contain fun activities or reinforcement work. Over time, you can even customize them to students' interests and levels.

- If you have easy access to a DVD player, start a collection of school-appropriate movies related to your subject.

- Keep a stack of workbooks to hand out for extra practice.

- If students keep journals, give them a "Things to Write About When I'm Stuck" paper or make up a topic based on your most recent activity.

- Come up with a few generic assignments that can apply to any topic: write a summary, draw a diagram, write and answer ten teacher-style questions, and so on. Keep extra copies of directions so you can reapply the idea without re-explaining.

TAKE OUT A BLANK PIECE OF PAPER...

Occasionally you need to fill ten to twenty minutes of class time with no materials or time to prepare. These activities aren't necessarily silent, but they can be adapted for most age groups and subjects, and they keep kids' attention. They can also be incorporated into future lesson plans if students enjoy them. This is a starter list: You will add to it on your own as you gain experience.

- **Story chains** Have each student take out notebook paper and begin writing a story. After a few minutes, tell kids to stop and pass their papers to the person behind them. Keep the chain going for as many rounds as necessary. Then return the stories to the original authors. If there is still time left, ask for volunteers to read.

- **Mental math** This activity doesn't even require a piece of paper. You talk. Kids do the problems in their heads: "Two...times four...plus six. Raise your hand silently if you think you know the answer... Okay, what is it?" Everyone can answer at the same time, so the whole class gets to participate. The trick is to give problems that are challenging but still simple enough for kids to do in their heads.

- **Alphabetical categories** Have students write down each letter of the alphabet on a sheet of paper. Then give them a category that relates to your subject: authors, countries, elements, and so on. Ask them to come up with a related word for each letter. The first one to finish wins, but the real winner is you, because kids will be concentrating at their desks instead of throwing paper.

- **Four-square review** Ask students to fold their paper into four sections, then give one mini-assignment for each square: draw a picture of a new concept, list synonyms for a word, list the achievements of an historical figure, and so on. Folding paper distracts kids from the fact that you just gave them four assignments.

PLANNING FOR A SUBSTITUTE

If no one has told you how to plan for a substitute, the day after your first absence can be an unpleasant wake-up call. The rule to remember is this: no one will do your job, your way, in your absence. Most subs won't teach a lesson for you even if you leave a fabulous, clearly written plan, so don't use up a great lesson on a day you won't be there to teach it.

It's up to you to let kids know what you expect from them when you're out. Threaten, promise, or plan a quiz for the day you return to encourage good work and behavior. If possible, ask the teacher next door to check in. Expect that somewhere between twenty-five and seventy-five percent of what you planned will actually be accomplished. Come back ready to follow up on reports of misbehavior.

While substitutes won't always be as responsible as you want them to be, it's still up to you to do the right thing. Do *not* leave anyone in your room with no clue who your students are or what to do with them. If you do this, good substitutes who know their rights will refuse to come back to your class. The ideal sub plan involves quiet work kids can do without much help. It uses materials that are easy to find or laid out in advance and backup work in case kids finish early. If you want this stranger to keep your class calm, cool, and collected, give him or her the tools to do so.

Most schools require teachers to make emergency substitute folders and leave them with the principal's secretary. Even if it's not required, it's a good idea to prepare a folder with the following things inside:

- A class list for each class you teach.
- Any relevant seating charts.
- Information on how to take attendance.
- Three simple lesson plans with backup activities and directions for finding materials.
- The names and locations of other adults who can answer questions.

15
OBSERVATION INFORMATION

HOW TO STAY READY FOR COMPANY

Many veteran teachers will tell you the best way to prepare for an observation is to "always teach like you are going to be observed." This sound bite seems like fabulous advice until you start teaching thirty-five hours a week. The truth is even the best teachers have moments when they are glad no one's in the room taking notes. However, there are some basic things you can do to stay ready for company.

1. **Teach kids how you want them to act when other adults are in the room.** The first time a visitor comes, kids will realize you don't want to reprimand them in front of company. Thus, they may behave like fools. Remain calm until the visitor leaves, then double the ordinary punishment for acting crazy. Be sure to choose a whole-class punishment that makes everyone unhappy. If the class behaved well, compliment and reward them. Your goal, in the beginning of the year, is to leave kids with a sense that when an outside person is in the room, you are still watching them. Reinforce this every time a visitor walks in by addressing the class's behavior as soon as the door closes.

2. **Have paperwork on hand.** Be prepared to show a grade book, lesson plans, and selected student folders at any time to anyone

who asks. Not only does this make you look organized, it also eliminates the chance for students to get rowdy while you dig through file drawers. If someone asks you for one of these things and it's not available, offer to bring it to your post-observation conference.

3. **Don't stop teaching when someone walks in.** Yes, it's hard to act natural while someone stares at you and writes on a clipboard. Your visitor already knows this. Say hello. If it feels right, introduce the visitor and ask the kids to greet him or her. Act confident that you are qualified and prepared. Then do what you came to do: teach.

4. **Explain the activity if necessary.** If an observer comes in at a moment that looks bad out of context, start talking. Don't wait for the observer to ask why a movie is playing, the kids are yelling, or you're sitting in front of the computer. Administrators will often give you the benefit of the doubt if you have an explanation—unless they come in another day to find a movie playing, kids yelling, and you sitting in front of the computer.

5. **Don't ask your principal for feedback.** Some teachers complain they have never been observed for more than five minutes and would like some feedback. Stop saying this. In fact, stop thinking this. The last thing you want is written feedback that results from nagging an administrator to be more critical of you. If your principal comes in for an observation and then leaves in five minutes, it means he or she is busy and has seen enough to decide you are doing your job. Be happy, be quiet, and, if you still want detailed feedback, ask someone who isn't your boss.

HOW TO PREPARE FOR THE DOG-AND-PONY SHOW

Observations scheduled in advance are usually longer and scarier than unannounced visits. During formal observations, it is hard not to go into sweaty-palms-try-not-to-drop-things-hope-your-kids-act-like-they-learned-something-this-year-and-the-kid-in-the-corner-stays-in-his-seat-with-his-big-mouth-shut mode. Principals and supervisors come to your room expecting a five-step lesson plan. They want to see that students are being accurately assessed and have mastered what you are teaching. These people know that you know you are being observed and expect to see your best work, which brings us to what my mentor teacher used to call the dog-and-pony show. Of course, you should always teach to the best of your ability. But when you know company is coming, you can line up the dogs and ponies in advance.

For formal observations, administrators generally use a checklist from the school district. They evaluate you according to "professional performance domains," which are explained for your convenience in a printer-friendly 180-page document available on the district website. Of course you will want to read this page-turner cover-to-cover to fully appreciate why the form says "Clarifies pedagogical content and expected cognitive performance on learning tasks" instead of "Gives clear directions." In case you haven't had time to review the standards, make it as easy as possible for observers to give you a high score in the following categories.

Lesson Planning

- Write objectives and homework on the board in advance.
- Make sure that your lesson plan is professional-looking and activities match objectives.
- Use a solid lesson that is impressive but not out of character. The last thing you want is a room full of confused students saying, "Hey, what do we do with all this science equipment?"

Classroom Management

- On observation day, warn students there will be someone watching the class. You can let them know you're being evaluated, but only if you are sure they will pull together to help you. If you have doubts, say the person is coming to evaluate *them* or to compare their class to other classes.

- Have materials ready to distribute quickly and quietly.
- If there are routines or activities you'd like to show off, work them into your lesson. Don't be afraid to remind students of proper procedures in front of the observer if you think it's necessary.
- Avoid rowdy or hands-on activities your kids haven't done before. Trust me. Your class's first debate or first experience with glitter should be a private affair.

Relationship with Students

- Give positive reinforcement that is as specific as possible and encourage student participation.
- Call on as many different students as possible. If you have a system for picking kids randomly, use it—but be ready to bend the rules if only one student knows the answer.

Teaching Style

- Speak with authority and loudly enough to be heard.
- Show you know your subject matter.
- Make directions as clear as possible. Repeat and rephrase if necessary.
- Be clear about why students need to know what you're teaching. Explain how it relates to past lessons and real life.
- Help confused students, but don't spend too much time at one desk.

Higher-Order Thinking

- Ask questions that require more than a one-word answer. Observers want to see that you are not sticking to yes-or-no questions or just telling kids the answer and saying "Right?"

- Make questions as deep and thought-provoking as you can without confusing the kids. If you ask a question and your class turns into the Blank-Stare Olympics, "randomly" call on a student likely to know the answer. Some teachers even admit to planting answers or reviewing material the day before. Remember, performing under pressure is hard for students too.

Assessment

- Describe your grading criteria for the activity or pass out a rubric that describes how the activity will be graded. You may also want to describe this in your lesson plans.
- Walk around the room as students work. Stop at desks to answer questions and check progress. This should improve student behavior and give you something to do with all that nervous energy.

ONE LAST NOTE

Don't start your observation-day lesson until your observer walks in. He or she may not show up on time—or at all. While teachers must prepare for scheduled observations, administrators sometimes miss them to handle unscheduled emergencies. It is a horrible feeling to start your dog-and-pony show on time and keep looking at the door only to have someone walk in just as you finish and have nothing impressive planned. Observers usually want to see a lesson from start to finish, so there's nothing wrong with working on something else until they arrive. When the person walks in, calmly end your other activity and start the show.

WORST OBSERVATION STORIES

If your observation doesn't go well, remember you're not the only one.

"*An administrator said I didn't know my subject area. Two years later, the same administrator asked me to teach advanced placement classes.***"**

"*My school had two reading coaches who visited my class almost every day. They would ask me to stop class or question me in front of students, and I felt the situation was bordering on harassment. I asked my mentor teacher for help. She said, 'These people are teachers just like you. Don't act like they're your bosses.' Then she told me to find work for them to do instead of bending over backward to be nice. The next time they came to my room, I asked them— politely of course—to dig through their files and make me a copy of some old test scores. I said I needed them for a review activity. Then every time they came to check my progress, I said, 'Yes, I'm doing fine. Did you get a chance to get those test scores?' I was a little less polite about it each time. Eventually both coaches stopped coming by completely. They never did get me the test scores, but that was okay. I didn't really need them in the first place.***"**

"*I was tardy on the day of one observation. I had been out sick the week before, so the class was a mess. It wasn't pretty.***"**

"*This lady from downtown came to my class with a checklist and tried to catch me up on all these petty details. She wrote it 'concerned' her that my students weren't grouped by ability. I wanted to say, 'Look, lady, I group my students by violent tendencies first, then by how much they talk. If I don't take care of those things, their ability won't matter much.' Instead, I just said, 'Thank you for your feedback,' and reminded myself that no one would ever look at that form again.***"**

"*Our school was on a list of low-performing schools, so we were under the microscope quite a bit. Sometimes it got ridiculous. There was one day I had six visitors at once in a class of nineteen kids. This lady we called 'The Snoopervisor' came first to warn me district people were on their way. She***

wanted to show off for them, so she stayed and pretended to help my students. Then a counselor brought in a university researcher, and they stood in the back of the room and whispered. Finally, two district people came in. They walked down the rows of first-graders with their giant shoulder bags, asking kids questions and looking through files for 'evidence of implementation.' My principal walked in a few minutes later to see why so many other people were in the room. Each observer rattled off his or her own version of, 'Don't mind me. Just keep doing what you're doing.' I tried to teach my lesson like everything was normal, but it was getting harder. Then the door opened again and it was another district person, stopping by to talk to one of his coworkers. This was my breaking point. I told the kids to put down their pencils and fold their arms on their desks. Then I turned to the adults and said, 'Y'all need to go.' I thought I was going to get in trouble for this, but no one said anything about it. I think they realized how ridiculous the situation was. **99**

16
TESTING, TESTING

> *High-stakes tests are a reality and, regardless of your personal sentiments on them, they are a hurdle your students must jump to graduate from high school. In that vein, do everything you can to help them pass. You have your college degree and time to pontificate and debate the meaning and validity of standardized tests. Your students don't.*

PREPARING FOR STANDARDIZED TESTS...SINCE YOU HAVE TO
From Day One

Most of your professional development will probably focus on combining test prep with meaningful instruction. I won't chip away at the iceberg of advice, except to say if testing is a big deal at your school, *do not* ignore it. Ask other teachers how they prepare. Use what you can from professional development. Teaching a tested subject is a constant challenge to creatively expose students to test-like questions. Luckily, you are not alone in this battle. The billion-dollar workbook industry is here to help you.

One Week Before the Test

Use your last week to do some review and build your students' confidence. Kids already have most of the knowledge they'll be working with, so offer encouragement even if you feel unsure. Teach relaxation techniques and remind students to take care of little details that can affect performance. Remind them to get a good night's sleep, eat a healthy, non-sugary breakfast, and wear layers of clothing in case the room is cold.

Test Day

The best thing about test day is that the kids are usually perfectly behaved. Some teachers bring students good-luck presents like apples, water, mints, or lucky pencils. This is up to you. At this point, you've done all you can, so wish your students good luck and tell them you believe in them. Now it's their turn to stress out.

THE PURPOSE BEHIND STANDARDIZED TESTS

My freshman year in high school, I had algebra first period. Most days our teacher, Mrs. W., didn't arrive until the last five minutes of class, leaving our class alone with no substitute. Eventually I realized my first period was a joke and started coming to school later, and one day, as I was getting off the bus in the middle of first period, I saw Mrs. W. Apparently she wasn't late enough, though, because she crossed the street and went to Dunkin' Donuts. Don't get me wrong—I thought this was fabulous at the time. But later, instead of taking a more advanced math class, I got stuck in remedial algebra.

Luckily, I didn't have a teacher like Mrs. W. teaching me to read, but not every student is so lucky. One purpose of standardized tests is to light a fire under lazy teachers. Slackers rob students of their education and make the rest of us look bad, so why not? Most of us would agree that teachers should be held accountable for doing their jobs, principals should answer for the teachers they hire, and students should be held to certain standards of knowledge. On paper, testing seems to do all of the above.

WEAKNESSES AND UNINTENDED CONSEQUENCES OF STANDARDIZED TESTS

Whether standardized tests live up to their intended purposes is already the controversial subject of many books, so it won't be the subject of this chapter. However, no one denies that, despite the intentions behind them, high-stakes tests have some built-in weaknesses and unintended consequences:

1. **Some students are so much below grade level that tests don't show whether they've improved.** It's hard to see progress on a grade-level test when kids are so far behind that their scores are similar to guessing. Even teaching to the test doesn't work when kids don't fully understand the questions and answer choices. It hurts to force students to take a test seriously when they don't have a good chance of passing.

" *When I graded my ESL kids' pretests, I wanted to curl up in the fetal position. The scores were so low I couldn't even use them for diagnostic purposes. One of my students was mentally retarded—he understood that he had to fill in the answer-sheet circles, but didn't know they represented answers to questions. This student scored higher than almost a third of my class. I ended up throwing out the tests.* **"**

2. **Students who don't perform well on standardized tests constantly get the message they are stupid.** We've learned about multiple intelligences. We know kids can be smart in ways that don't show up on tests, but try telling that to a teenager who may not graduate high school because he can't pass the state reading exam. Tell that to a third-grader who spends a whole year failing practice tests and is so nervous she throws up on test-day morning. The higher we raise the stakes, the more these tests take a psychological toll on the kids who don't pass.

❝ *The most depressing day of my first year was when I had to give summer school notices to students who didn't pass the tests. I tried to break the news in the most private, upbeat way possible. In return, the kids tried not to look too heartbroken. One student, who got nervous on tests and had been in summer school every year since first grade, just grabbed the notice off my desk and said loudly, 'Yeah, I know. I failed.'* ❞

3. **Students who can pass the test feel like they are superstars, which is not necessarily true.** All the hype surrounding these tests makes us forget that they are only basic, subject-area skills tests. After hearing nonstop about their importance, students who pass can get cocky, especially if they succeeded easily while classmates struggled.

❝ *The implication that test-passers are smart enough to slack off is a disservice to them and to their teachers. It also keeps standards just one level above test questions and leads to the disturbing attitude that once 'The Test' is over, learning is done for the year.* ❞

4. **Teachers are encouraged to replace real teaching with test prep.** When we focus full-time on testing, we suggest critical-thinking skills are a luxury most public schools can't afford to provide. Instead of working on students' reading skills, we teach tricks that might help them pass a reading test without being able to read. We also forget that every day spent on tests, benchmark tests, practice tests, practice-test review, and test-taking strategies or attending test "pep rallies" is a day *not* spent preparing students for success in college or life. The pressure to look good on paper forces us to treat students like hot potatoes: as long as we can get them to pass our year's exams, we will never be blamed for their failure. We just hope that when their lack

of real skills catches up with them, they will be in someone else's hands.

" *One month before the test, my principal started sending the assistant principal to subtly hint that we should 'put extra focus' on the tested subjects. We already knew this because everything about the school pressured us to teach only the tested subjects. We should have known it wouldn't end there, because there was nothing subtle about our principal. She didn't believe other people understood things unless they were clearly stated and then repeated a million times. Three weeks before the test, she started getting on the PA and reminding us to focus on tested subjects. Then she just gave up and started giving long speeches where she would say things like 'Third grade: that means you are only teaching reading. That's reading, third grade! Fourth grade, math and reading. Math. And. Reading! Fifth grade…' and so on. She did this every morning for two weeks while parents were in the school dropping off their kids. If I were a parent and heard some of these speeches, I would have pulled my kid out of that school.* **"**

5. **Test answers are sometimes ambiguous.** Answers shouldn't be obvious to test-age kids, but they should seem straightforward to adults who specialize in the tested subject. Sometimes even teachers find themselves confused by poorly worded questions or answer choices.

" *We reviewed using a released test from the previous year. One story was about a so-called typical American family, with a mother who told these really corny jokes. You could barely tell they were supposed to be funny. My students didn't laugh, and neither did I, but the correct answer on the test said the mother's character was 'playful and humorous.' Two of the questions related to this opinion. One of my students asked, 'Who writes these things, anyway?' I felt this test was actually biased against kids who had a good sense of humor.* **"**

6. **Other factors affect test scores.** High-stakes exams test a lot more than what students have learned. They test how much sleep kids got the night before, how well they perform under pressure, and whether other issues are distracting them. They also test whether a student takes the test seriously or rushes through and then falls asleep. Some tests count toward a school grade but are not graduation requirements for kids. In these cases, scores reflect which students skipped the test completely and went to the beach.

❝ *The state is replacing paper tests with computer-based tests, but our school does not have enough bandwidth or high quality computers to make this work well. As a result, we often have situations in which computers shut down and erase kids' answers, or students miss an hour of the test while we wait for our IT guy to resolve technical difficulties. This is hard even on strong students, but when students are already struggling, a computer shutdown can shut them down as well. Students who had to take the same test twice often tell teachers that they 'just filled in whatever the second time around,' which is a scary thing to hear when our jobs might depend on their scores.* **❞**

7. **There is lots of cheating and pressure to cheat.** Teachers are often left alone on test day and pressured to "get results." The following year's teacher gets a class full of kids who passed the test but don't have the skills to succeed in a new grade. On top of this, the kids believe teachers will always "help" them on the day of the test, so they aren't very motivated. Then, if the new teacher is honest, it looks like students went backward from the year before.

❝ *It was common knowledge at my school that if you wanted to keep your job for the next year, you would make sure X percent of your students got a* *passing score on the state test. Teachers would openly share cheating tips with one another. One popular strategy was to look over the shoulders of a few top students and then compare their answers to those of a student at risk of failing. If the answers were different, the teachers would nudge the low-performing student and whisper something like, 'Check number thirteen.'* **"**

8. **Test prep makes both students and teachers hate being at school.** What lessons do you best remember from your own school days? Experiments? Performances? Projects? Answers may vary, but it's probably safe to say no one's fondest memories include strategies for eliminating incorrect answer choices. Many of us got into teaching hoping to share the fun, creative, and inspiring lessons we once enjoyed. Instead, the rumbling of the oncoming test keeps our schools in a constant state of emergency. Fun activities are pushed out of the curriculum because they're not the most efficient way to cover tested material. Teachers feel guilty because we're not giving kids the educational experience we'd hoped to. The kids, on the other hand, don't know exactly what they're missing. They just know school isn't much fun.

" *The day before the test, I felt like a plane that was not going fast enough to take off. Most of my students were still failing the practice exercises. I was going over some test-taking strategies on the overhead projector, desperately hoping this would get them where they needed to be. I looked around the class, and everyone looked completely spaced out except one little girl who always followed my advice but failed anyway because she had dyslexia. I was so unhappy I could barely lift my arm.* **"**

9. **Performance anxiety turns schools into the twilight zone.** Test pressure interferes with the regularly scheduled program for at least

a month before the actual test. The more your school panics about performance, the more it feels like you have entered another dimension.

“_Every year, we have this disturbing 'beat the test' pep rally. We pull kids out of class during their last chance to review so they can watch fourth- and fifth-graders in cheerleading outfits that show off their underwear. My boy students always look really happy, but I don't think it has much to do with the motivational cheers. At the end, they call up the teachers and give us each a balloon. I try to act excited, even though the whole thing kind of makes me want to cry._**”**

17
GRADING WORK WITHOUT HATING WORK

"My son was already in high school when I started teaching. I had so many papers to grade, I brought them everywhere, including to one of his important track meets. I finished my stack of quizzes and was feeling great when my son ran up to me, 'Did you see me, Mom?' I hadn't. I had been so busy grading that I missed his big moment."

WHY GRADING IS SO FRUSTRATING

Today you really are going to grade those papers. (If all your papers are already graded, you can skip this chapter. And I hate you.)

You know it's important to keep up with grading, but lesson planning can't wait until tomorrow, faculty meetings leave you emotionally drained, and you don't want to break promises to call parents. You start saying you will grade at home, but there are distractions and you are tired. Your car has become the ungraded-paper express shuttle as you take home your constantly growing pile and bring it back untouched in your Office Depot "Star Teacher" tote bag or one of those rolling crates that seemed like such a good idea at the time. But today is the day. After all the delays and excuses, you are ready to get back on schedule. You take a deep breath and tell yourself it shouldn't be so hard, once you get started…

The first paper you read irritates you. Some of it is done correctly, but this student clearly didn't put in much effort. He needs to know that you know he is being lazy and can do better. However, you resent that your comment explaining this is probably taking longer than he spent on the whole assignment.

The next paper you pick up has so many mistakes you are not sure what to correct. You don't want to discourage this girl by covering the whole page with negative comments, so you try to find something positive to say to balance out each correction. ("Nice job indenting your paragraphs! Great adjective!") You are not sure if you should give a grade that honestly reflects the horrendous quality of the work or a grade that will show this girl her efforts mean something.

Then you get something that is halfway decent as a piece of writing but has nothing to do with the directions. You start to cherry-pick the parts that do follow instructions so that you have something positive to say. After all, the kid should get credit for trying, but he also needs to know that directions *are* important and *will* affect his grade. The work could use a few other corrections, but you decide it is more important to focus this student's attention on following directions.

Finally, you get a neat paper that shows understanding of the assignment, directions, and concept. It is such a relief to your eyeballs you want to just slap an A on it, but then you start to wonder, "Are my standards already so low from those first few papers that anything decent looks like A work? If I give this child an A, will he stop working as hard?"

The next paper is a pretty clear B. There are a few corrections, but the work shows a basic understanding of what you taught. You are excited to see that most of this student's mistakes follow one simple pattern. The right comment from you could turn him into an A student...or her? There is no name on the paper! Hopefully he—or she?—will come ask you why he—or she?—didn't get the assignment back. You write a note explaining that no-name papers automatically lose ten points. Then you put it in a separate pile to remind yourself the grade has not been recorded.

Two papers later, you see the same paper, word for word, written by someone else.

You already have a small headache. It gets worse as you move on to the next paper and try to decode handwriting you can only suspect covers up some type of intelligence. As you write "Please be neater!" at the top, you feel like one of those teachers who you thought were so picky about handwriting when you were in school. You always hated those teachers. You force yourself to squint through the assignment and find something good to say, although you also add one more comment about sloppy writing. You give the paper a grade that seems fair, considering your headache…

Only 267 more to go.

WHAT EXPERIENCED TEACHERS KNOW ABOUT GRADING

❝*I had gotten so behind on grading, the oldest assignments in my pile were over a month old. I felt I had to grade them before addressing newer work, but I knew there was no chance I would catch up. Overwhelmed, I explained my situation to a teacher in my department. His advice started, 'Now, see, you should never throw out student work in your classroom garbage…'***❞**

Grading is an important part of our job. It's also the part most likely to cover our kitchen tables, ruin our weekends, and never, ever be finished. Experienced teachers with up-to-date grade books will tell you the secret is to do it right away so you don't fall behind. Maybe they really follow this advice and are not just saying it to make you cry. Chances are, though, they also know these things:

- You don't have to write comments on everything you grade.
- You don't have to grade every paper the kids turn in. Some assignments are just for practice.
- Usually, if no one gets a minor assignment back, kids won't ask for it.
- Students can sometimes help with grading.
- Many grades are at least partly subjective, and students don't know if you had trouble deciding a grade.
- One grade won't make a huge impact on a student's average. It's not worth your time to obsess over the difference between a B– and a C+.
- You can sometimes grade papers while students work independently.

THE OTHER PURPOSES OF GRADES

In theory, grading lets both you and your students know whether they learned what you taught. Students get valuable feedback from your comments. Checking progress regularly lets you reteach and provide individual assistance. Assessment informs instruction. That's why it's built into the five-step lesson plan you always follow…right?

In reality, many of us get behind on grading. We realize students are failing when it's almost report-card time. We find out weeks too late that no one understood our fraction-pizza lesson after all. We spend Saturdays feeling guilty, Sundays repeatedly correcting the same careless errors, and Mondays finding graded papers on our classroom floors.

Why does it seem like we're constantly behind on grading? Part of the answer is simple math: ten minutes worth of detailed comments per paper on 150 high school essays equals twenty-five hours of grading time. The same goes for grading thirty elementary students' work in five different subjects. Even one minute per assignment adds up to two and a half hours—and students do more than one assignment each week. District memorandums remind us that students need "specific, constructive, meaningful" feedback, and this is true. It's also true, however, that most of the grading you do will not be perfect. If it is perfect, it probably will not be done.

To keep things in perspective, remember that even imperfect grading serves a purpose. This was true when we were students, and it's still true now.

Grades provide a reward system for academic work. As much as we want kids to learn for the sake of knowledge, we know we'd better have a few outside incentives. The promise of getting a grade is already built into the school system, so it's one wheel we don't have to invent ourselves.

Grades are the simplest way of communicating with parents and future teachers. Signals can get crossed when communicating with parents, but nothing gets to the point faster than a simple letter grade. Likewise, teachers at a child's new school will look at his transcripts—not your comments on his last book report.

Grades fill up your grade book. Most school districts require a minimum of two grades per week, per child, per subject. That's more than one hundred grade-book columns each quarter that you won't want empty near report-card time.

MAKING GRADING FAST AND FAIR

"*My second year, I promised myself to stop taking papers home. I usually didn't touch them anyway and just ended up feeling guilty. Instead, I started grading at school until a specific time each day and leaving empty-handed. This cutoff point forced me to use my time at school more wisely and made me a more effective teacher in the end.***"**

Grading should reflect the quality of student work, but it should also be time-efficient for you. If you spend more time grading work than your students spend doing work, you are guaranteed to stay behind. Tricks for fast, fair grading vary by subject, but the following ideas should help as you find your own strategies.

Shave Grading Time Off Each Assignment

- Grade only part of the assignment. Tell students which parts you will grade only after they turn in their work.
- Grade even or odd problems only. Many textbooks test each skill with two or more problems.
- Wait until after essays are done, then pick from a bag of essay parts (introduction, first body paragraph, etc.). Grade only the paragraph you picked.
- Focus on revising one section of a project. Then grade it for improvement.
- Tell students to underline the details you're looking for: vocabulary words, transitions, order of operations, and so on. This will make your job easier and focus students on following directions.
- Have students keep work in a folder you check weekly or a notebook you check every ten entries.
- Squeeze more than one grade out of complicated assignments (research grade, in-class progress grade, final draft grade, presentation grade, etc.).
- If you teach more than one subject to your class, assign cross-curricular projects and count the grades for multiple subjects.
- Make assessments ten, twenty, or twenty-five questions so that you can calculate percentages quickly.
- Use short-answer or multiple-choice questions for assignments you need to grade quickly.
- Ask another teacher if your school has a Scantron machine.

Watching a machine grade two hundred tests in sixty seconds is a beautiful feeling. Learning about this machine after you hand-grade two hundred tests? Not so beautiful.

Save Time on Writing Comments

- Give most grades quickly. Focus on a few students each time who need more detailed feedback. Put their papers back at the bottom of the pile after you assign them a grade. You'll be able to give them more attention once the entire stack of papers is not staring at you.

- For major assignments, have rubrics or checklists with premade comments (e.g., "Quotations are cited correctly: 10 points"). Explain these thoroughly on the front end, then circle the numbers next to them as you grade. If you find yourself getting sidetracked and writing additional comments, grade with a highlighter.

- Create a premade blank rubric for daily assignments. The directions might say something like, "In order to get a C or above, your assignment must be _____ pages long and follow these basic requirements: _____. In order to get a B or above, you must highlight and label five examples of this skill: _____. In order to get an A, your paper must be free of errors in _____." Students can fill in the blank parts of the rubric with specific directions that you write on the board each day.

- Develop systems that let you assign grades by checking students' papers as they work. Students like getting immediate feedback, and you can make comments in person while they still have a chance to fix mistakes.

- Buy stamps for comments you make often. Many teacher supply stores have stamps for handwriting, incomplete work, and no-name papers. As you collect work, you can sometimes stamp unacceptable papers and hand them back immediately.

- Spend time in the beginning of the year teaching your students what you expect in their answers. After focusing on the process for a while, you can concentrate more of your feedback on whether answers are correct.

- Review common mistake patterns as a class instead of writing the same comment on twenty papers.

Make Some Grades "Instant"

- Skim some assignments for effort, completeness, and understanding. Then quickly assign a grade and move on. The official-sounding name for this is "holistic grading."
- Occasionally give free grades to everyone who did an assignment, especially for homework. This is also a built-in effort grade, so it will encourage struggling students to keep doing their work.
- Keep extra copies of your seating chart or class list. Sometimes you can walk around the class with a clipboard, spot-check kids' work, and write their grades on the chart. This gives you a full column of grades without papers ever touching your desk.
- Use your class list to give a four-part daily grade. Students get twenty-five points for attendance (ten if they come late), twenty-five for preparation (and/or homework), twenty-five for participation (including behavior), and twenty-five for completing class work (which you can spot-check at the end of class). Partial credit is possible for all categories, but should be either ten or twenty-five points so that you can calculate grades quickly.

Plan Around Grading

- If you assign a major project on a novel and then watch the movie, make the project due before the movie. Movie time for your students can be grading time for you. This idea applies on a smaller scale also. You can plan to grade during any period in which kids will be busy and quiet for twenty minutes without needing your help.

- When the class is working on an essay or test, arrange for students to work or read silently at their desks if they finish early. This buys you some grading time. Even more importantly, it keeps slower workers from feeling rushed as their classmates finish.

- If you teach more than one subject, space out the due dates of major assignments.

- If looking at a huge stack of ungraded work makes your stomach drop, divide papers into stacks of ten—finding time to grade ten essays is easier than finding time to grade 150.

- If you know in advance that an assignment is just for practice, place it in a separate file. Throw it away after a month or so if no one asks about it.

- Make a schedule and set aside specific times to grade.

- Know what type of grader you are. Can you fill tiny spaces of free time by grading two or three papers, or do you need uninterrupted silence? Do you need a deadline to motivate you? Can you grade during lunch? TV commercials? Faculty meetings? Be realistic and plan around your own capabilities.

Have Students Help

- Although peer-grading comes with its own set of issues, students can sometimes grade each other's work as you review answers. If you teach more than one class of the same subject, give out papers from another class.

- Students can sometimes grade their own work, especially on multiple-choice assignments. Have students circle their final answers in crayon so they can't erase answers as you review. Another possibility is for students to put all pencils away after a quiz then grade with a pen or marker. Students with a pencil on their desk during review time fail the quiz automatically.

SOME THOUGHTS ON PEER-GRADING

Having students switch papers is a compromise—you are giving students more opportunity to cheat, and they are giving up some of their privacy. The payoff is less paperwork for you and faster feedback for them. Peer-grading saves time and can even be educational when done right, but let's be honest: there is no substitute for feedback from a college-educated teacher. It is up to you to find an appropriate balance between peer-reviewed work and work graded by you. The following are some things to keep in mind:

- Some written work is meant for your eyes only. Give students the option of grading their own work or handing it directly to you if answers are personal.

- Peer-grading needs to be taught like anything else you want students to do well. Before turning kids loose on each other's work, grade a sample paper as a class.

- Tell students if they think a paper was graded unfairly they can write "Please recheck" at the top and put it in your in-box.

- If students will be putting grades on their friends' work, there is a built-in incentive for them to bump up the score. It helps to start the year with an explanation of why it is important to be honest. Then add that if a grader cheats to help a friend, both students fail. Two days after your first peer-graded quiz, say something like, "I'm not going to name names, but I had to tell two students they failed this quiz for dishonest grading. I hope this won't happen again." Look very disappointed.

WHAT TO DO WITH GRADED WORK

Get graded work off your desk and out of sight as soon as possible. Put it in a basket to file or hand out at the appropriate time. Students can help.

OH, S#*T! MY FIRST SET OF GRADES IS DUE TOMORROW!

Many teachers clearly remember a moment right before their first report-card day when they realized there should have been 2,700 grades in their grade books. Instead, many of us—I mean *them*—had about ten recorded grades, seven crates of ungraded papers, and few options that would let them respect themselves in the morning. If you are in this situation, let me start by saying you can never, ever, *ever* let this happen again. Promise? Okay. There *are* some desperate measures you can take if grades are due tomorrow and there is no chance you will catch up. These are not recommended, but they are one step more ethical than making up random grades to keep your job:

1. Double up legitimate assignments under different titles. This will keep grades somewhat accurate.

2. Record any graded work you have not already added to your grade book.

3. Separate the crates of work into assignment-related piles. Keep the piles that you think best represent your kids' work.

4. Eyeball the papers in each pile and put grades on them as quickly as possible. No comments.

5. Repeat this process as necessary until you have enough columns in your grade book to satisfy district requirements and your own conscience.

6. Skim final grades to see if any seem unfair, inaccurate, or unlikely. Adjust accordingly. (Hint: this is a good time to give students the benefit of the doubt, especially those who may challenge a grade.)

This process will take several painful hours. Every fifteen minutes or so, take a moment to feel depressed, ashamed, and guilty. Promise yourself not to be such a horrible, irresponsible person in the future. Now go! What are you waiting for? Your grades are due tomorrow!

18
MOMENTS WE'RE NOT PROUD OF

The first year of teaching is like the first year of anything: we learn the lessons today that we needed yesterday, and we learn them the hard way. Few of us chose this career expecting an easy paycheck. None of us hoped to make students feel discouraged, disinterested, or disrespected. We never planned to fail. In fact, many of us pictured ourselves becoming outstanding teachers who would one day inspire a movie, hopefully starring someone hot (sorry, Edward James Olmos).

We came to be the solution to what's wrong with education. Understandably, our worst days are those that make us feel like part of the problem.

When I first started interviewing teachers, I asked, "Have you ever had a day that made you feel you were horrible at your job?" The answer was always the same: "One day? Please. I've had too many to count."

Eventually, I changed the question: "Can you describe *one* day that made you feel like a bad teacher?" The following are some of the answers I received:

"*I came back from being out and was still a little sick. My classroom was a mess and the first thing students told me was that they missed the substitute.***"**

❝Because of low student enrollment, I was transferred from my first teaching assignment just when I was getting the hang of it. My new school had no discipline system in place, and the class I took over was being managed by a behavior specialist because their first teacher had quit. Among other things, students would climb out my first-floor window and tell me they were sending themselves to the office because they didn't agree with my instructions. When they got there, the principal's secretary would hug them and give them candy.**❞**

❝Most male teachers don't teach kindergarten, but when school started, I found myself in a classroom filled with five-year-olds. An art teacher had made me two beautiful, hand-painted bathroom passes, and one of my little charges lost one. I was furious and screamed at the boy for having been so careless. My voice must have been pretty loud, because the next day, my principal casually mentioned that he had heard me all the way in the main office. If I could have dug a hole and jumped in at that very moment, I would have done so. That incident, thank God, was never mentioned again, but I learned an important lesson about controlling my anger.**❞**

❝I was teaching a high school media class and jumped at the idea of involving my students in a class project: developing, casting, rehearsing, and filming a script. I should have worried when the kids created a story about a substitute who faces the class from hell. Need I say more? When the day of shooting arrived, someone suggested we all put on our coats and film outside. Then one student thought it would be cute to climb the flagpole. Without asking permission, he shimmied up the pole and yelled at me to start filming. Then I heard my principal screaming at my back, 'What is going on here!?' As I turned to explain, my class clown started yelling at us from the top of the building, 'Hey, get this shot!' I screamed at him that he was in big trouble, but it turned out he wasn't the only one. I never taught media again.**❞**

❝I put down a student in front of the class. He made me so mad, I said some things I knew as a teacher I shouldn't have said. I apologized to him later.**❞**

"Halfway through a parent conference, I realized I was talking about the wrong child. By the time I figured it out, there wasn't much I could do to cover up the mistake. The good news is this woman's daughter was doing much better than the girl I was talking about at first. She was so relieved she forgot to be mad at me."

"I had a student who spoke no English at all. He spent most of his time drawing and trying not to fall asleep. I knew he needed me to work with him individually, but with thirty-three other students, I often overlooked him. One day, we wrote an essay as a class. He copied the whole thing from the board, even though he didn't understand a word. Instead of complimenting him on writing his first page of English, I pointed out a mistake with his indentation. His eyes just dropped to his desk. I tried to backpedal and tell him I was proud of his work, but he wasn't buying it. The damage had been done. From that day on, I made more of an effort to pay attention to this child and praise his efforts. Over time, he learned more English, and I learned to choose my own language more carefully."

"My school focused so much on the tested subjects that social studies were pretty much eliminated. I was struggling to keep my head above water, so I let it slide even though social studies had been one of my own favorite subjects. One day, my students, who were mostly Mexican and Salvadoran, had a chance to participate in a Hispanic heritage poster contest. They had two questions: 'What does Hispanic mean?' and 'What does heritage mean?' That was definitely a day I felt I was failing as a teacher."

"I lost a kid during a field trip. We had to page him at the museum and almost missed our bus searching for him. It turned out he had snuck back to the gift shop to buy a toy and then couldn't find the group. After my heart started beating again, I took the toy and made his mom come get it. I didn't say anything to the principal, though, and was glad no one else did either."

66 *One of my honors students turned in a poem that was absolutely brilliant. I suggested she submit it to our literary magazine, which I was in charge of. I also sent it to a district-wide poetry magazine, which subsequently published it. After I shared this magazine with my English department, a fellow teacher approached me and showed me the same poem in an anthology of Langston Hughes's lesser-known works. To say I was embarrassed would have been an understatement. Luckily, no one from the district said anything, and I began a more thorough study of Hughes.* 99

66 *I had worked out a system where my third-graders went directly to their seats after our bathroom break instead of lining up in the hallway. They were to immediately begin their reading passages, so as not to waste any 'learning time.' I got a little cocky. During one break, I called over a more experienced teacher to show off my quietly working students. I rambled about my new system with growing confidence until we both heard a commotion in the boys' bathroom. The teacher excused himself and came back holding two of my boys, both covered in soap and water. Enough said.* 99

66 *I once dreamed of being a tattoo artist, but I worried I would mess up and someone would have to live with my mistake. Instead I became an art teacher. One day, a second-grader muttered something rude under his breath while I was talking to him. I followed him outside the school at the end of the day and talked to his father, who slapped him so hard it would have made a bigger kid cry. The boy didn't even move. He just looked at the ground. His little sister was standing there and had been covering her eyes since I started talking, like she knew this was going to happen. I was the only one who didn't see it coming. On that day, I wondered if I would have done less damage as a tattoo artist.* 99

66 *Not long after I finally got discipline under control, I mistakenly took my fourth-graders to lunch an hour early. They went into the cafeteria in a nice straight line, so I didn't follow them. My vice principal paged me about two minutes later,*

and I ran back to find my students sitting on the stage in a lunchroom full of kindergartners. I let them laugh at me for about a minute. Then I said, 'Okay, get over it,' and tried to teach a normal lesson. Later I apologized to my assistant principal and mumbled some excuse involving daylight savings time. **"**

"I bought a Porsche my first year at an inner-city school in the early '70s. That turned out to be a bad idea. I was an overnight hero with everybody, and people began to question whether I was a drug smuggler. Rather than keep up the image, I sold it to a collector. I got me a shiny, new Ford pickup, and my Porsche days were over. **"**

"By January of my first year, I thought I knew my troublemakers. My seating chart limited interaction between feuding students, and I thought I had a good idea of what was going on at all times. However, nothing prepared me for the day I spent my planning period creating posters only to have them splattered with blood. It seemed like a typical afternoon. I was helping a group of eighth-graders with their class work when a commotion started in the back of the room. It was between two of my 'good' kids, but I could tell by their tone that neither young man was simply making threats. I looked in the hallway for a security officer. It was empty. By the time I turned back around, I saw blood. One student had stabbed the other with a broken pen, and the wound was so deep it needed stitches. I quickly began handing out tasks: go find the dean, keep the boys separated, get the custodian and tell him to bring bleach and a mop, use desks to create a barrier around the splattered blood. Although I felt I had handled the crisis well, I couldn't understand how a fight between two studious children could have escalated so fast. I cried in the car on my way home and had to pull over to regain composure. To add insult to injury, the children completed their suspensions and administrators put them both back into my classroom! **"**

"One fifth-grader who was supposed to be going to resource (special ed) during a portion of the day was actually hiding in the bathroom smoking. I *had no clue. The resource teacher thought she was with me, and I thought she was with the resource teacher. She did this for almost a month before someone finally caught her.* **"**

"*I started teaching in the 1940s as a home economics teacher. We collected food and made baskets for the soldiers' families during World War II. One day while I was teaching, some girls in the back of the room ate the donated food. I was furious, but one of the baskets had a whole container of prunes in it, so the girls got what was coming to them in the end.* **"**

"*By the end of my first year, I felt like the kids respected me, so I started acting and dressing more casually. Summer was coming, and the weather was getting hotter, and one day our air conditioner broke. This was a computer class, and we had thirty computers heating up the room. The kids didn't want to do anything. I gave up on my lesson and tried to play a trivia game, but all they wanted to do was whine about the heat. Finally I just said, 'Quit bitchin' about the weather so we can get something done.' Since I had cursed, the kids took it as a green light to curse and started calling people bitches. There was one girl in particular—the kids had been picking on her all year. She was big for her age—way bigger than anyone in the class, including me. She had short hair, and one of the boys kept calling her a bald-headed bitch until she reached her breaking point. The last time she told him to stop, it was clear that she wasn't playing. The kid stopped for a minute like he was thinking about it, and I held my breath hoping he would shut up. Then I heard, really softly, 'Bald-headed fat beeyotch.' This girl jumped up, pushed all the computers off one of the tables, and started running toward the boy. I tried to grab onto the back of her shirt, but she was bigger than me and I was wearing flip-flops. I ended up getting dragged behind her like a Superman cape as she chased this kid into the hallway. Of course, the rest of the class wanted to see a good fight, so they followed us, and other classes started coming out to see the action. Luckily a large male teacher from next door had heard the commotion. He was able to restrain the girl as soon as she left the* *room. After everything calmed down, the principal came into the class to find out what had happened. My students were all there, and I felt like I should take responsibility, so I admitted that I might have started the problem by using the word bitch. He said, 'What? Are you serious? It's not like you said fuck!' The kids just stared at him with their mouths hanging open. I loved that principal forever after that.* **99**

I wanted to end this chapter with advice on how to avoid low points, but I can't. All teachers have bad days. Rookies have them more often and take them more personally. Longtime teachers, on the other hand, have stored enough good memories to reassure themselves and balance out a few disasters. In fact, the teachers who contributed to this section all chose to keep teaching, in spite of these incidents…and if that's not an argument for the rewards of this profession, nothing is.

19
DOS AND DON'TS
FOR HELPING
NEW TEACHERS IN
YOUR SCHOOL

*I*t's like the old saying goes: give a man a fish, and you'll feed him for a day. Teach a man to fish, and you'll feed him for a lifetime. Tell a man fishing is easy and any idiot could do it, make fun of his fishing equipment and style without offering any help, eat the fish you caught in front of him and talk about how delicious it is, and you won't have to worry about whether the man starves. He will probably just jump off the boat.

Yes, we've all been there, and new teachers have to pay their dues. Maybe *we* learned the hard way and no one helped *us*. Maybe we did everything right from the beginning. Maybe we already *told* the new teacher next door *exactly* what he needs to do and he didn't *listen* to us. Hey, we're busy with our own classes.

There are plenty of great reasons why we don't offer our newest coworkers the support they need, but most teachers agree that nothing in our training prepared us for the sink-or-swim reality of the classroom. Fifteen percent of new teachers don't make it to the second year. Nearly half quit within five years. Students at high-poverty schools are also much more likely to have a beginning teacher at the front of the classroom. If we don't look out for each other, no one else will look out for us.

The job of a mentor teacher often feels like this:

1. Give new teachers advice you know is true.
2. Watch them act like they already knew it and then do it wrong or not at all.
3. Help them clean up the mess they made without saying "I told you so."
4. Repeat as necessary until they learn everything you told them the hard way, just like you did.
5. Let them know they are doing a great job.

Helping rookies is frustrating sometimes. They can be cocky, whiny, hardheaded, or all of the above—just like we were. New teachers may not admit it, or even know it, but they need us. It is often our support that keeps the great teachers of the future from quitting before they realize they will become great.

The following table contains a few tips, straight from the rookies themselves, on how to help your newest coworkers.

Do	Don't
Do introduce yourself and let beginners know where they can find you.	**Don't** talk about them behind their backs or go public with their private concerns. If you have offered yourself as someone who can be trusted, take that responsibility seriously.
Do make sure they know the correct procedures for attendance, referrals, and other paperwork.	**Don't** nitpick everything they do. *"My first day, the office called for my attendance cards twice within fifteen minutes. They used the PA so all my students heard me get yelled at. I had to stop class and scramble to alphabetize the cards. Then the office sent them back because I hadn't put a rubber band around them."*
Do let them know how discipline problems are—or *aren't*—handled by the school. For that matter, try to warn them about any unpleasant surprises before they find out the hard way. *"Several teachers at my school pressed their emergency buttons for the first time only to find out they didn't work. I was one of those teachers, so I can say from experience it would have been nice to know this before I desperately needed security to come to my room."*	**Don't** be overly negative about your school or students. It can make new teachers feel hopeless or defensive. Rookies may also feel like they should shield kids from your comments instead of being open about their frustrations. *"When I first started teaching severely emotionally disturbed students, other SED teachers wanted to give me all the background on each kid. A lot of days, I would go home depressed just from hearing the stories."*

Do	Don't
Do make extra copies of materials that work for you. The best resources are those that teachers can photocopy or use as is. Computerized lesson plans and forms are also helpful—the basics are done, and adjustments are easy to make. *"Another science teacher shared some tried-and-true experiments with me, with detailed instructions and all the worksheets I needed. This was a lifesaver. I made some changes over time, but starting with everything in order was awesome!"*	**Don't** encourage rookies to be lazy teachers. Keeping someone from wasting effort is different from saying, "Just give the kids enough worksheets to keep them quiet."
Do make sure they are invited to faculty social events. Feeling like part of a community is important. Feeling like an outsider when everyone else is part of a community is painful.	**Don't** let them sit alone at every meeting or talk past them in the teachers' lounge. Treat new teachers the way you would want your class to treat a new student.
Do remember that new teachers are under the microscope much more than experienced teachers. They get observed and critiqued all the time. If you really want to help them, offer an opportunity to watch *you* teach.	**Don't** act too much like you think they are struggling. New teachers are often extra-sensitive, even to well-meaning comments. *"My grade-level chair told me, 'Don't worry. I don't tell anyone you're having problems in your class.' She was a sweet person and didn't mean any offense, but all I could think was 'Uh-oh, why does she think I'm having problems in my class?'"*

Do	Don't
Do help them prioritize paperwork.	**Don't** let rookies miss deadlines with serious consequences while sweating over work that no one else takes seriously. It can be hard for them to separate urgent documents from those that can wait.
Do tell them what they can do tomorrow instead of what they should have done yesterday. None of us have control over the past, and obsessing about mistakes demoralizes rookies.	**Don't** preach what you don't practice. New teachers have already heard lots of advice that looks good on paper. Now they need practical, realistic, honest answers. Don't just say "Be consistent" or "Keep up with grading." Share your own strategies for doing these things. Otherwise, you're just being mean.
Do occasionally take tough cases off their hands. Some troublemakers are experts at reading inexperience and can ruin the chemistry of a class. A break from the distraction gives rookies a chance to regain confidence and get other kids on their side.	**Don't** reprimand their students in front of them. It doesn't help them gain their students' respect. It helps *you* gain their students' respect and suggests they can't do the job without you. Plus, it's only one step away from the most obnoxious line in education: "They would know better than to do that in *my* class." Save that for someone you hate— or someone you want to hate you.

Do	Don't
Do act like you expect them to become great one day. The great teachers of the future are often hard on themselves the first year. Let them know you see that spark in them. Also, tell them if you used one of their ideas or think they did something well. Some rookies do start off on the right foot from the beginning, and they deserve to hear it. *"At the end of my first day, I was exhausted and knew I had made so many mistakes. My mentor teacher said, 'The first day is always hard, but I can already tell you have what it takes to be a wonderful teacher.' There were so many days when I thought back to that comment for encouragement."*	**Don't** treat them like you expect them to be gone next year. *"At new-teacher orientation, they spent two hours telling us the many ways we could be fired. When I got to school, my classes were in the computer lab, and my department head made a huge deal out of property control. He made it seem like my job was on the line if any computers were damaged. This lab was also used for a night-school class, and many mornings I came in to find computer parts missing. I spent the whole year wondering if I should send out résumés."*
Do understand that they are under a lot of stress. Remember your own first year? Sharing lessons you learned the hard way will inspire new teachers and let them know they're not alone. *"I had been to several workshops that emphasized 'learning centers.' When I tried to implement them in my overcrowded classroom, the kids went nuts. There was another teacher who had centers in her room, so I asked her how she made them work. She said, 'I don't. I did them once and it was a disaster. Now they're just for decoration.' This probably sounds bad, but I can't tell you how relieved I felt when I heard that."*	**Don't** act like teaching should be easy from day one or put new teachers down to make yourself seem better. *"I finally found a positive reward system that got my students to behave. A teacher I worked with saw this and told me, 'I don't believe in bribing students to act right.' This was a woman who knew I was struggling for most of the year, and that was the only advice she ever offered."*

ROOKIE TEACHER TIPS FOR ADMINISTRATORS

Schools that don't provide for new staff become training grounds for other schools. Beginners stick around long enough to get certified and then transfer or quit. It can be tough to identify problems sometimes, because only the most vocal or confident rookies speak up when they're unhappy. The following suggestions are really tips on how to treat all teachers, but they are extra important for making your school a rookie-friendly environment:

- **Be honest about what resources your school can provide.** Veteran teachers know that you often have to wait for supplies or permission. Rookies plan around your promises and tend to take all rules literally. They are disproportionately hurt by school-wide bottlenecks such as copy machine restrictions that keep copies from ever getting made or signature requirements from people who are almost never in the building. Choose your words carefully around rookies and only promise what you can deliver soon.

- **Let teachers know what, where, and who they will be teaching as soon as possible.** Beginners need lots of prep time to start the year with confidence. They also need advanced warning to be ready for major changes.

- **Discuss concerns in private.** Criticizing new teachers in front of colleagues makes them targets of teachers'-lounge gossip. Reprimanding rookies in front of students is even worse—it makes them seem weak and sends them back to class with destroyed credibility.

- **Back up teachers' decisions whenever possible.** New teachers face extra challenges from students, and they worry about parents questioning grades and consequences. Knowing they'll have your support during a conference gives them more confidence in the classroom.

- **Assign reliable mentors.** Not all mentors are created equal. Do your best to choose hardworking, discreet, understanding teachers whose classes are similar to those of their trainees.

- **Let them know what you think they are doing well.** Your opinion matters a lot to new teachers, whether they show it or not.

- **Have a fair system for distributing students with behavior problems.** Under no circumstances should veteran teachers be allowed to switch students into a rookie's class. Filling a new teacher's class with their colleagues' unwanted students is unfair to everyone in the room.

- **Buy them this book.** Before you give it to them, take a look at the chapter about principals (Chapter 13).

20
MAKING NEXT YEAR BETTER

*E*ven after you've made it through your first year, you have some work to do. For one thing, you need to pull out that "Ideas for the Future" file. Summer is your time to review all the revelations that came one lesson too late. Another idea, if you think you can handle it, is to give your students anonymous surveys. After thirty-six weeks, no one knows what kind of teacher you were better than they do. Administrators visited your class a few times. Your students were in there every day.

Yes, I am using the term *every day* loosely here. Yes, a good number of surveys will come back with answers like "Let us watch movies and don't give homework." Still, most kids will be honest, and many answers will be helpful. Put the surveys in a folder. Tape it closed. Promise not to open it until school lets out and report cards are printed. A few answers may sting, but at least you won't repeat the same mistakes for years without noticing.

This survey is your chance to ask students the questions you've been asking yourself all year. The following are a few possibilities:

- What was your favorite/least favorite thing about this class?
- How did your behavior, attendance, and effort in this class compare to what you did in other classes?

- Do you feel you were treated with respect? Please describe any incident where you felt disrespected.
- Do you feel you were recognized when you worked hard or did something well?
- What could your teacher have done to help you learn better?
- What could your teacher have done to make sure all students learned better?
- If you became a teacher, what would you do differently? What would you do the same way?
- Did anything important happen this year that the teacher didn't notice?
- What will you remember most about this class?
- Please write and answer one other question that should have been on this survey.

Once you have surveyed the kids, you need to ask *yourself* some questions. In your case, they don't need an answer right away. The important thing is to keep asking them every year.

- How can I organize my time to get more out of each day?
- How can I organize my class in a way that lets kids help me run it effectively?
- How can I avoid making last year's mistakes in the future?
- How can I get students to learn more of what they need to know?
- How can I make myself a better person so I can become a better teacher?
- How can I balance teaching with the rest of my life so I can stay motivated and enthusiastic over time?

That's right. The last chapter in this book is about end-of-year surveys and looking through a box of old papers.

Are you satisfied with this ending? Of course not. That's because deep down, you still wanted teaching to be like the movies. We all do. We all want great lines that come on cue and become turning points in students' lives. We all want that moment on the last day when our toughest kid turns to us with tears in his eyes. There's supposed to be a sign that we are the hero of this story and we will never wonder whether we're bad at this again.

Instead, we end the year tired and still unsure of ourselves. Even if this were a movie, the last day would make a horrible freeze-frame. Decorations are down. Kids are more interested in hanging out with each other than in expressing gratitude to us. The only soundtrack comes from the radio we let them play so we can handle paperwork in peace. We don't always end the year knowing what we did right.

Don't feel too bad, though. Your job isn't to end every year with a grand finale. It is to keep asking questions, grading quizzes, sitting through meetings, trying to catch up on paperwork, and walking students to the bathroom—slowly becoming a better teacher in the process. There is no parting scene, only everyday duties. And once in a while, there are moments—unplanned, unexpected, and unexplainable—when you know you've made an impact whether tomorrow is a good day or not. You are the teacher you came to be right now. Cue the music, and let the credits roll.

Make Me or Break Me
by Roxanna Elden

They say this first year will make me
Or break me.
I guess that's because it takes me
Eight days to get through a stack of papers.
And there are eight more waiting,
And every day I stay at school later

And get less done…
This is *not* fun.
Help me someone!!!

I'm already counting the number of Mondays
Until vacation
(There are twelve, by the way,
And I'm getting impatient)
Because I spent all last night
On grading and preparation
But I can't get these kids to just
SHUT UP!!!
And take this inspiration.

My temptation to keep driving
Instead of arriving
In the teachers' parking lot
Is almost as strong
As my fear of what could go wrong
If I don't pull into this parking spot
And I'm not sure if I can take it…

I'm trying so hard to make it work
The way the movies make it seem.
I've been sacrificing so much sleep
I forgot what it feels like to dream.
This isn't the person I'm used to being
Not the image of me I'm used to seeing

I miss the days when I was a student,

Complaining about teachers to my friends…
This job seemed so easy from the other end.

From here, nothing looks the same,
And you know what's even more of a shame?
I hear my teachers' voices
When I yell my students' names.

And you know that one quiet girl,
In the back,
With the glasses?
I overheard her mom saying
She wants to change classes.

They say this job is rewarding, but lately
I just feel like all my students hate me…
Their papers frustrate me
And I'm going so crazy
No sane person would want to date me.

But I'm here to stay.
It takes a lot to break me.

And that's why I say
No matter what it takes me…
This year
Is gonna *make* me.

THANKS

This book was made possible by the honesty and generosity of the following people:

Lillian Acevedo-Brako
Maipu Aguila
Cory Allen
Ashli Andersen
Andy Baldwin
Eric Berry
Andrew Block
George Bombalier
Tara Brock
Meghan Casey
Manny Cruz
Tanya Das
Crystal Davis
Shawn DeNight
Zakia Dilday
Billie Diehl
Luther Dollar III
Rosa Elba
John Ermer
Tara Garland
Ana M. Gonzalez-
  Fernandez
Reem Hamdan
Nichola Hanson
Damita Haynes-
  Ferguson

Taryn Hendrix
Bianca Huff
Diana Hurtado
Panitra Jackson
Valerie Jean-Gilles
Maite Jerez
Deno Johnson
Sibel Kaplan
Dr. Alice Kawazoe
Cathy Kelly
Dr. David Kirsner
Lorenzo Ladaga
Tamica Lewis
Billy Lombardo
Jon Mangana
Daniel Desnudo
  Martínez
Herminia Martínez
Iris Martinez
Victoria Martínez
Jodi Mcbride
Sarah McFarland
Kristine McMillan
  Willford
Stephanie Millar
Katia Mompoint

Delphine Opet
Abena Osei
Carmen Paredes
Brian Perry
Chris Pickett
Monica Redondo
Griselis Reyes
Eric Richey
Maria Salazar
Sharon Samuels
Joshua Sheridan
Lavanya Star-Fulton
Sarah Thom
J. F. Thompson
Darlyn Trujillo-
  Espinosa
Stan Walker
Phyllis Williams
Ed "Coach Woody"
  Woodson
Terri Woltch
Rosena Wright

Other contributors who, for various reasons, asked that their names not be used.

ALSO, THANKS TO...

- **Rita Rosenkranz:** For being everything I hoped for in a literary agent. For seeing the big picture from the beginning, and catching all the little details along the way.
- **Michael Sprague and Tim Brazier:** For helping this book to its feet.
- **Suzy Bainbridge and the team at Sourcebooks:** For helping this book find its way.
- **Arielle Ekstut and David Henry Sterry:** The authors of *The Essential Guide to Getting Your Book Published*. Your amazing book and workshop helped me do just that.
- **Brenda Orr:** My first-year mentor teacher, always fabulous and never completely retired, who told me after a rough first day that you saw a great teacher in me.
- **The faculty and administration of Hialeah High:** For making the school a great place to work. Special thanks to the coworkers who trusted me with their stories.
- **Reem Hamdan, Daniel D. Martínez, Zakia Dilday, Abena Osei, Tanya Das, and Billy Lombardo:** For sharing your time, stories, and comments.
- **Ginger Seehafer and Inga Aragon:** For turning my words into pictures and losing nothing in the translation.
- **Grandma Barbara, Grandma Sylvia, Grandpa Harold, Aunt Wendy, Uncle Marty, Uncle Stewart, Stephanie, Tammie, Bryan, and Rudy:** For being a great family, for reading the book, for advice, help, company, good times, and furriness...not necessarily in that order.
- **Claude-Henry Volmar:** For marrying me in spite of various annoying writer-habits and making my life better in every way.
- **Erica Elden Dewsbury:** For everything. No other way to put it. Without you, there would be no book.
- **Phyllis Mandler and Gary Elden:** My first teachers, who did for me what I hope to do for my students—led by example, expected the best, and repeated the most important lessons until they sunk in.